JESSICA LANGE

JESSICA LANGE

A Biography

J. T. JEFFRIES

ST. MARTIN'S PRESS • NEW YORK

Design by Paolo Pepe

Library of Congress Cataloging in Publication Data

Jeffries, J. T.
    Jessica Lange.

    1. Lange, Jessica. 2. Moving-picture actors and
actresses—United States—Biography.   I. Title.
PN2287.L2834J44   1986   791.43'028'0924 [B]   86-1957
ISBN 0-312-44200-9

First Edition
10 9 8 7 6 5 4 3 2 1

CONTENTS

There's a need for aloneness which I don't think most people realize for an actor. It's almost like having certain kinds of secrets for yourself that you'll let the whole world in on only for a moment, when you're acting.

—Marilyn Monroe

JESSICA LANGE

1

LIVES OF A BLONDE

The political radicalization of great American actresses seems to exist in inverse relationship to the idiocy of their first roles. Sally Field played Gidget and a Flying Nun; Jane Fonda was Barbarella. And Jessica Lange was the girl in King Kong's fist. That hardly any of the public remembers the bimbo origins of these now Academy Award-winning fixtures is due in large part to the actresses' own efforts to erase them, in roles of earnest battles between right and wrong.

In the fall of 1984, for example, Lange co-produced and starred in *Country*, the story of a contemporary Iowa family struggling to keep their farm. In Iowa, farmers saw the movie and wept. But the movie failed in the rest of the country, unaided by a bevy of respectful, if unemotional, reviews. The problem was not just the difficult subject matter: the apparently unstoppable, insoluble destruction of the American family farm. Nor was it the competition from two other films released that same fall about struggling farmers, in what came to be called the "Dust Bowl Trilogy" films: Mark Rydell's *The River* and Robert Benton's *Places in the Heart*.

No, the problem was that Lange miscalculated the nature of her appeal. Now, if Lange had made a film about a blonde movie star who visits Iowa to find that farmers are being

1

pushed off the land, and, while fighting for their cause, meets and falls in love with a sexy Pulitzer Prize-winning playwright who also happens to be a movie star, thereby forcing her to leave her world-famous, gorgeous ex-lover of a ballet dancer— now *that* picture would have sold tickets.

Because Jessica Lange *is* a movie star, in the good old-fashioned sense of the word. Her talent and skill belong to a particular order, whether she wants them to or not. She is not, arguably, the consummate actress of her generation (that mantle generally being borne by her only rival, Meryl Streep), the most versatile or gifted, the most prolific, even the sexiest. But she has, as Jack Nicholson, her co-star in *The Postman Always Rings Twice* (1981) put it, that "huge female appeal." Without necessarily wanting to be, Jessica Lange has become consecrated as the blonde American goddess of her generation. After a decade of hard-edged boy-beauties, forgettable nymphets, or strident feminist actresses, she stays in people's minds. Here, at last, is an actress worth lusting after.

No wonder many sophisticated moviegoers reacted to *Country* as if it were something Lange had made up out of a Norman Rockwell painting. Sally Field, Sissy Spacek, Jane Fonda —let them doff the faded cotton dresses, lose the makeup, carry the politically correct roles. Alone among these women, Jessica Lange lives as pure image. She bears the mantle of an icon unique to American cinema: the blonde movie star. The slim number of roles on which she built her reputation reads like a roll call of blonde archetypes. They read, in fact, like legends within legends—for each new part referred not just to the fictional character itself, but to actual other actresses, with legends of their own, whose fates reflect on hers, so tightly are these players bound in their parts. She was the new Fay Wray, the new Lana Turner, the real-life actress Frances Farmer, the

Marilyn Monroe-like bubblehead in *Tootsie*. Handed time-worn, clichéd approaches to femininity, Lange breathed the breath of an independent, contemporary woman into these encased blonde icons and became the first sensual, thinking woman's blonde.

Fay Wray played the original blonde girl, Kong's victim, love, and downfall, in the 1933 *King Kong*, and her part, beloved by movie fans for generations, became legend. Her short name rhymed so that no one forgot it—but only because of *Kong*, for, although she made dozens of other movies, she was never in anything else that anyone but hardcore film buffs ever heard of. In 1976, when Dino De Laurentiis announced a national talent hunt for the part for his big-budget remake—Barbra Streisand, Cher, and numerous others having turned it down—the joke was obvious. It was the first of Jessica's inherited actresses in a part: the first, the most insidious, the potentially most painful. From the start, Jessica Lange was not merely the screaming blonde in a giant ape's hairy palm—she was Fay Wray, heiress to notoriety and fifteen-minute fame. Take the part and welcome oblivion. Play Beauty to the Beast, the ultimate male-female paradigm. Hardly anyone can be taken seriously when she plays the love object of an ape.

When Lange starred in *King Kong*, she was widely perceived to be as phenomonally stupid as her character, Dwan, in the film. Her career appeared to go nowhere for two years afterward. Little known, however, is that her own sex appeal in *King Kong* impressed three major directors at the time, all of whom would remember her in *King Kong* when it came time for casting far more serious roles: Bob Fosse, who put her in *All That Jazz* (1979), Bob Rafelson, who would cast her in *The Postman Always Rings Twice* (1981), and Sydney Pollack, who thought of her for *Tootsie* (1982).

Lange made no more films until 1979, when her onetime lover, the prolific and talented Broadway director and choreographer Bob Fosse, wrote a part expressly for her in his autobiographical extravaganza, *All That Jazz*. Although a film that few people associate with Lange's career, it instinctively grasped her capacity as Blonde Icon—and Fosse cast her as precisely that. She was Angelique, the Angel of Death, a near-motionless creature of beauty wrapped in white gauze, a White Widow spider who casually enlightens her victims as she ensnares them. Fosse based the character on his interpretation of Lange in his own life, as someone who could take him or leave him, who was hip to his tricks—a Greek Chorus, a muse, beauty incarnate. When no one else would hire Lange, this was the only part she could get, playing a Freudian angel to a real-life lover.

Then came her breakthrough—the role that made the critics sit up and take notice: her murderous Cora to Jack Nicholson's Frank in Bob Rafelson's 1981 version of *The Postman Always Rings Twice* (a little domestic comedy, *How to Beat the High Cost of Living,* needs mention only in passing—it opened and closed in a week in 1980). It was, in a sense, her debut film—she herself called it that—and every actress in Hollywood wanted the part. Landing this most coveted role, Lange instantly inherited another actress in a part. Now she was the new Lana Turner, the quintessential two-dimensional glamour girl, the Sweater Girl who had represented the classiest version of sleek blonde sexiness in a less clinical era. Turner never had a more memorable role than in the 1946 version of *The Postman Always Rings Twice* with John Garfield (a movie Lange refused to see during the shoot). The question was: Could this young woman, still widely perceived as little more than an unremarkable starlet, make them forget Lana Turner? She did more—she made them forget Jack Nicholson. Lange filled in James M. Cain's Cora by letting loose with an exhausted, pressing want. This was sex as both escape and trap, expressed with her hands, her eyes, her body. STUNNING JESSICA IN LANA ROLE read one headline. "Jessica," wrote Andrew Sarris, "is a revelation." The movie fell far short of expectations, but Jessica Lange, learning to land on her feet after several years of practice, saw her stock soar.

What does great beauty do to men—something they will die or kill for, the desire that takes men out of the realm of their usual self-protection—that was the theme in these first roles. Lange's Cora growled, "I'm tired of what's right and what's wrong," in a way that made men forget what right and wrong were in the first place. ("Hey, pal, I saw her," cracks the lawyer at Nicholson's bedside. "*I* might kill for her.") She was beauty that contained within it, by definition, destruction for man or beast—the orgasm at the end of the line. Beauty—she knows what it does to men and she forgives them for it. She knows what she uses it for and forgives herself for it.

Recent female sex symbols seemed unlikely to inspire that level of obsession—yet Lange clearly did. Lange had a real woman's body, not some skinny, aerobic tautness, but good-sized thighs, a torso you could get lost in, and the best eyebrows in the business. "Few are the men," said Nicholson aptly, "who don't want to fall at her feet."

But in *Frances*, the legend flipped. It was a look in the mirror, a real-life parable of the destructiveness of beauty not for men lured to their doom, but for the woman with the face to lure them there. Rarely has a more chilling true story come out of Hollywood than that of Frances Farmer, a talented actress, badgered by studios in the thirties, of her betrayal by and the deliberate cruelty of her mother and, finally, her violent decade-long entombment in mental hospitals, where she was the victim of bizarre psychiatric treatments. Frances Farmer's life came to symbolize, for many who encountered it, Hollywood at its cruelest, its most inept, and there were few actresses in that town in 1981 who wouldn't have given half a career to play the part. When Lange got the role on the strength of *Postman*, her task was not to replace a legend but to create one: the Blonde as Victim. Though the script was a confusing and ultimately insulting portrait of the incarcerated Paramount star, Lange somehow transcended its limitations. She astounded the critics again—and again in a movie that was universally panned and another failure at the box office. Lange played this part with some kind of hatred in the corner of her eyes, a gesturing hopelessness in her too-large hands, a pent-up rage let loose at being a woman chained to an empty fantasy of blondeness for her identity and punished for trying to escape it. Lange knew. She played Frances with a ferocity that left fellow actors in the dust. She illuminated the dark side of the blonde myth. Rage borne of having been a Hollywood pawn herself, rage for the woman, all women, who knew better than her image, lashed out of the screen. This time, the beast was Beauty, with a capital B. The lexicon had been added to by one.

Within a week of *Frances*'s unveiling in Manhattan to qualify for the Oscars—and garnering Jessica her first of three Best Actress nominations—*Tootsie* went into wide release for 1982 Christmas audiences. As the film's ultimate object of adoration, Lange proved as enchanting to Dustin Hoffman in *Tootsie* as was Marilyn Monroe to Tony Curtis when she played the innocent bubblehead in another famous comedy in drag, *Some Like It Hot. Tootsie*, a film Lange did almost as an afterthought, turned out to be the final seal on her status as Blonde Legend, for she was now, in the person of the soap opera star Julie

Nichols, truly Tootsie, the blonde cutie desired, not by King
Kong, but by every American male who saw the movie. And
there were many who did, for *Tootsie* took in $94 million at
the box office in 1982 alone, to become one of the best-selling
comedies in Columbia Pictures' history. It remains her only hit
film and, of four Academy Award nominations, the only one
to provide an Oscar, for Best Supporting Actress in 1983.

Lange, in fact, is the only actress who can be considered a
superstar on the basis of one certified hit, six commercial, if not
critical, failures, and at least one financial disappointment of
her own production. No matter. So saturated are we with the
history and lore of our most beloved images, we can ignore
quantity in exchange for the rare quality of the instantly recognized icon, filling something like a permanent niche in the
public imagination.

Beauty is not an easy thing to survive. It is the most forgettable, the most fleeting of powers. Automatically painted on by
every man or woman who sees her, the beautiful woman's very
presence is freighted with assumptions and expectations that
go back to the farthest reach of fables. The beautiful woman
is a walking myth, the only woman in every movie. For such
people, life and legend are the same. The dumb blonde and the
doomed blonde—they're the same people, played in succes-
sion. Destruction is inherent in the part. Lana Turner the
Sweater Girl becomes Lana Turner pleading for her daughter's life in the murder trial of her gangster lover. Marilyn
Monroe is inseparable from her suicide. The two legends unite:
The blonde American sex goddess is created to be destroyed,
like some virgin chosen to be sacrificed to appease the Gods—
consecrated in film, destroyed in life, even before age could
destroy her looks.

Jessica Lange ranks as survivor of a harrowing legacy. That

first experience with *King Kong* must have warped her tremendously—what began as a welcome seduction quickly turned into a rape. Both her trust in others and in her own sense of judgment were severely undermined. When she finally emerged, in 1983, with her double Academy Award nominations and her Best Supporting Actress for *Tootsie*, her audience knew how far she had come, that she had made it on her own terms.

This is Jessica Lange's triumph. Her career ultimately reads against the legend. In the end, there is no such thing as a dumb blonde. Lange is the ditzy blonde who turned out to be all brains, she's the victim turned victor, the Blonde Icon for the eighties, but with a happily postfeminist appeal. She brings to women the ultimate luxury: to be sexual without being witless, to have at her feet the men she wants, not merely the men who want her.

It took many women of Lange's generation until their early thirties to get a good grip on their own sense of worth. It is something, after all, to be loved by two of the sexiest men in the twentieth century—first Mikhail Baryshnikov, dancer extraordinaire, and lover in an on-again, off-again six-year relationship begun shortly after *King Kong*, culminating, in 1981, in the birth of Alexandra (Shura for short), named after Misha's mother. Sam Shepard fell in love with Jessica Lange just as the nation's media were falling in love with him, so that this celebrated playwright-cum-movie star and his beloved actress, both supposedly publicity-shy and private, conducted one of the most publicized offscreen romances in recent memory. Lange, in these and other romances, resembles no one as much as that famous flame of the nineteenth century, Alma Mahler, who counted among her lovers some of the most illustrious minds of the century.

But to be loved, even by geniuses, is not the same as harness-
ing your own abilities, as being recognized for your own work.
Lange has both. This is the happily-ever-after woman in the
eighties. Her own work, her own babies, her own ranch, a
gorgeous boyfriend and the blonde legend is updated to the
first version that can appeal to a woman with intelligence.

It is precisely at this point, of having made it, in every sense
of the word, that Lange takes the icon in her own two hands
and offers up the Final Blonde Archetype in a film of her own
choosing. Who is she, really? Why, she's a farm housewife in
pink curlers, ladling out pancakes to a black-tie audience at the
New York Film Festival, a baby on her hip and receipts on the
calendar. In *Country*, Lange exercises the profoundest, most
elusive power our culture can offer an actor: the power to
create one's own image. And so Jessica Lange creates hers. It
is not a cynical one. On the contrary, this was, for Lange, the
equivalent of the hero's return, in classic Homeric terms. Having abandoned her native Minnesota as a rebellious eighteen-
year-old, she returns, at thirty-five, on celluloid, triumphant,
invigorated, wizened by the trials sustained as a stranger in a
strange land. She celebrates in film the kind of woman she
would have been had she never left home; she joins in fiction
the life she abhorred in reality. In the last entry in the Blonde
lexicon, Lange replaces Hollywood's values with the simple
Iowan integrity that a successful movie star can never claim.

So the Blonde Icon, having made it, retires. The image is
now her life; her movie roles, merely acting. In fact, in two of
her recent pictures, Jessica Lange is no longer even a blonde.
In Tennessee Williams' *Cat on a Hot Tin Roof* (1985) made for
the pay cable service Showtime, Lange plays red-haired,
honey-voiced Maggie (another reverberant role, of course, to
Elizabeth Taylor's). In *Sweet Dreams*, Karel Reisz's 1985 film

biography of the legendary country balladeer, Patsy Cline, Lange dyes her hair dark brown, walks around pregnant half the time and beat up the other half, and gets as close to ugly onscreen as those cheekbones are ever likely to get. Patsy Cline was nobody's fool, and about as far from the blonde icon as a character can get. She was eminently cheerful, sane, strong, and abundantly talented (Jessica lip-synched to Cline's recorded voice). Lange clearly relished playing this role. But once again, though her endearing, vivid performance won high praise and a third nomination for Best Actress, she couldn't save an uneven picture, another box office disappointment.

Most of us know Lange first as the movie star, so this biography works its way backwards—starting with the creation of Jessica Lange the star, which begins with the filming of *Frances* and moves to the present; then, to the struggles of making it, from her years as a freewheeling world traveler, waitress, and student of mime, to her casting in *King Kong*, to her arrival in *Postman;* and finally, to her childhood as youngest daughter in a family of three girls and a boy, the offspring of hardy Finnish, Dutch, and Polish settlers of the Minnesota Iron Range and a father who couldn't stay in a town for more than two years at a time.

Nowadays, Lange's private life celebrates the virtues of retreat from the rigors of her self-created celebrity. She raises her five-year-old daughter by Baryshnikov and baby girl (born January 13, 1986) by Shepard, breeds horses on her New Mexico ranch, spends summer and Christmas vacations in a two-story log cabin on 120 wooded acres in Holyoke, not far from her hometown of Cloquet, Minnesota (pop. 11,000), and occasionally emerges for media chores on either coast. New projects which appeal to her spring from the pens of blue-chip contemporary woman writers. She'll act with Sissy Spacek and Diane Keaton in the film version of Beth Henley's Pulitzer Prize-winning *Crimes of the Heart* in the spring of 1986. She also optioned Jayne Anne Phillips's *Machine Dreams,* for which Lange herself has completed the first draft of a screenplay.

Lange, like her lover Sam Shepard, plays the game best by appearing not to play it at all. This makes them the most American of their generation; they succeed in Hollywood's Babylon so they can rise to a powerful enough position to denounce it. For both, the worst fate is the anonymity of the Midwest into which they were born. To reject (or appear to reject) the fame they've sought and worked for is merely an extension of the abhorrence of their own rootless, hollow childhoods; this sacrifice is required of them in order to transcend it. Jessica Lange escaped from the grim emptiness of eighteen towns in as many years through imagining movies. After a point, however, the imagination requires an audience —and yet despises itself for needing one. The audience, for its part, doesn't like being reminded that that's all it is. Far better that the audience can participate in some way in the mystique of fame by latching on to stars who appear to disdain it. So, this former hippie who feared, more than anything else, the obscurity of her native Midwest, returns to the land on film and in Bruce Weber photographs. A contemporary legend in image land, finding her way in a desert of public selves and private passions. The blonde survives.

2

FRANCES

F ew people attempt the difficult livelihood of public displays of imagination. For the lucky, uncreative souls who
don't, it is hard to understand the extreme irony of a work that
defines one's life, extracts one's best, takes the largest toll of
what one consider's one's hardest effort, and yet remains, in the
public mind, nothing more than a curiosity, a minor work—
or, to the businessman, a flop.

Such was the case with *Frances* (1982). Not that the film
served Jessica Lange poorly. She got her Academy Award
nomination, her awestruck reviews, and the sweet satisfaction
of being taken seriously as an actress, as she'd craved for years.
Everyone would remember Lange as Frances. But almost no
one liked the film.

Lange leapt out from the screen as Frances Farmer in this
saga of the tormented thirties Hollywood beauty who starred
on Broadway and in films but fell to obscurity after years of
mental abuse. Farmer's left-wing politics and refusal to play the
Hollywood glamour girl were punished not only by the Hollywood establishment, who kept her in a series of B movies, but
by her own mother, who took custody of her and had her
imprisoned for ten years in the violent ward of a mental hospital in Seattle, Washington, where she was, by some reports,
finally given a lobotomy.

In a performance of "great intelligence," as one critic put it, Lange's Frances was never, for one moment, insane, and often appeared to be a lot more on the ball than anyone else in the movie. So powerful was her acting that it seemed as if she were the only actual live being in the film, and had been surrounded by life-size, stand-up paper dolls instead of other people. Even the performances of her supporting actors—Kim Stanley as Lillian, her mother, Sam Shepard as Harry York, her friend in need—paled in comparison to Lange's searing portrayal of the tortured star.

Nonetheless, *Frances* was an imperfect film. The reviews were scathing—critics were as universally disgusted with the movie as they were agog at Jessica Lange's performance in it. The story was contrived, critics said, slow, without dramatic pacing or logical motivations. To those critics, such as Rex Reed, who had followed the story of Frances Farmer closely over the years, the film was worse than bad. It was a betrayal. For the story of Frances Farmer was a parable of Hollywood at its cruelest, its most inept. Hers was the ultimate paradigm of woman as victim, and the truth of her story had been buried for years. Those who took it upon themselves to make such a film—and the year, 1982, saw several plays and films on Farmer's life—had a moral duty to do justice to this martyred actress's life. *Frances,* the most visible and lavish of the Farmer stories, failed critically and at the box office.

The puzzling thing is how a film like this could fall so short in the first place. For if ever a movie should have been good, *Frances* should have been. In a decade when most movies are aimed at twelve-year-olds, the subject was a meaty, tough as-signment, aimed at adults. As such, the film was a labor of love for everyone from the leading lady to the set designer. "There was a chance in a lifetime to do a picture like this," said the director of photography, Laszlo Kovacs. Richard Sylbert, the set designer, was simply the best in the business, having won Academy Awards for his work in *Chinatown* and *Shampoo*. The producers, the writers, the director—all knew every second of Frances Farmer's tragic life, all believed in a film that should, if anything, have vindicated her tragedy, somehow, by portraying some kind of truth about what she went through. There were not one, but two books, both with highly cinematic narratives, on which to base a film of Farmer's life—her own autobiography, *Will There Ever Be a Morning?* and William Arnold's gripping 1978 biography, *Shadowland*. *Frances*'s original producer, Marie Yates, had, in fact, first read *Shadowland* as an unpublished manuscript and optioned the film rights immediately.

But financing was not easy to get. Having optioned the book in 1979, Yates worked with Arnold and other associates for two years before she hooked up with Jonathan Sanger, who had just finished the critically acclaimed *Elephant Man* for Mel Brooks's production company, Brooksfilms. Sanger sold Brooks on the project, but, for reasons which have never been made clear, Brooks jettisoned Arnold's involvement and brought in two Oscar-nominated screenwriters from *The Elephant Man*, Christopher Devore and Eric Bergren (both later went on to write the 1985 *Dune*). Arnold and the other associates sued, and lost, finally, long after the film had been released in 1981.

Unfortunately, with William Arnold and his book out of the picture, the producers had to prove that their film was based on original material. The screenwriters came up with one Harry York, a largely fictional character who popped in and out of Farmer's life, rescuing her with the monotonous predictability of Rin Tin Tin. The existence of this character, "a figment of the writer's desperation," as Vincent Canby put it, had only one redeeming characteristic: Sam Shepard was cast in the part.

Brooks hired Graeme Clifford, an Australian film editor, to make his directorial debut on *Frances*. Clifford, an innovative craftsman who had moved from Australia to England and then to the United States, had done intriguing editing in films like Nicholas Roeg's thriller *Don't Look Now*, with Julie Christie and Donald Sutherland. At thirty-eight, he itched to direct his first film. Coincidentally, while editing Bob Rafelson's 1981 *The Postman Always Rings Twice*, Clifford, Pygmalionlike, had fallen in love with the beautiful face running through the Steenbeck editing machine. Jessica Lange, he decided, would be perfect for the part of Frances. Clifford had been a Farmer devotee for years and knew every detail of her life. Even before he had been chosen to direct the film, Clifford had insisted to Sanger and Brooks that Lange be allowed to read for the part.

Jessica herself had long known she'd make the perfect Frances. Years before, an acting teacher, Warren Robertson, had told her so. Teaching Lange in a 1974 acting class with several models in New York, Robertson had been struck by the "ferocity combined with innocence" in the acting of this lithe young woman. Two students, one of them Susan Blakely, read a dialogue from *Will There Ever Be a Morning?* between Frances and her vitriolic, manipulative mother Lillian. Fascinated, Jessica hunted for Frances Farmer's autobiography and read it. "It stunned me," she said. She learned more of Farmer's tragic story from Kenneth Anger's book on the underside of Hollywood, *Hollywood Babylon*. Then she searched for Farmer's best film, *Come and Get It*—a late-show special by 1974. "I was struck by her physical presence," Lange said. "I was struck by what I saw in her face and body." The identification was emotional, "nothing intellectual or rational, more a sympathy or empathy. She's a very identifiable character."

For Lange, the identification was instantaneous and complete. Even in 1974 and 1975, waiting on tables, struggling to become a model, Lange "somehow . . . knew I'd play her one day—and that was before I'd ever made a film." Like Farmer, Lange had deserted home for travels, arrived in New York to study acting, and was then plucked from obscurity by a Paramount contract that brought her west to Hollywood and seething frustration. Or perhaps it was Farmer's frantic and doomed desire to be politically useful and artistically important, two goals shared by Lange that Hollywood did as little to serve for her as it had for Farmer. Or, possibly it was Jessica's own connection to a "powerful and charismatic parent," namely, her father, Albert.

Later, when Jessica had made *King Kong* and was floundering somewhat for direction, back in New York, Robertson suggested she try to develop Frances Farmer's life story as a movie. Robertson had been in the Actors Studio, and "certainly remembered who Frances Farmer was." Warren Robertson and Jessica actually worked for several weeks on the emotional subtext of this character. "It was obvious that Jessica had all kinds of emotion pent up inside of her," Robertson recalled. He was "a little taken aback," he admitted, when she'd got the part in the film *Frances* and didn't contact him again. Susan Blakely, in turn, developed *Will There Ever Be a Morning?* as a made-for-TV movie.

Whatever the link, Jessica tried unsuccessfully for years to share her passion for the Farmer story. As her own career moved forward, she tried to cajole the directors she knew to direct Farmer's story with her in it. In New York, around the time of *All That Jazz*, she tried to persuade Fosse, but the overcommitted director turned her down. Two years later, in

California, she turned to Bob Rafelson as they worked on *The Postman Always Rings Twice* and was again refused. "Neither of them," Jessica discovered ruefully, "felt it was their cup of tea."

Ah. That's because they weren't among the converted. For years, a cross section of American film fans had been drawn to the story of Frances Farmer with all the magnetic intensity of an attraction to the Holy Grail. They had become converts, and several such converts, having met Frances each in their own way, converged on this particular project, which began as *The Frances Farmer Story*. Others, acting under the same influences, would join to produce a made-for-TV film, three off-Broadway plays, and a low-budget independent feature— all within a year of each other.

All were drawn to this tragic figure, as if the power, the dignity Farmer was denied in life could come back after death and claim its justice. Nothing about Frances Farmer was simple. Everything about Frances Farmer was complex and contemporary—her politics, her language, her aesthetic idealism (she was an early member of the Group Theater, starring on Broadway in the important Odets play *Golden Boy*), her quite probable lesbianism. Her inability to play the Hollywood game fit into a postfeminist, post-sixties Hollywood far better than it did in its own day, when the dream machine was allowed to run unquestioned.

Ironically, it was "out of the blue" that Lange got a phone call from Graeme Clifford. Up to that point, Sanger, Brooks, and Clifford had been sitting back as a veritable who's who of Hollywood's top actresses paraded before them: Diane Keaton, Jane Fonda, Goldie Hawn, Sissy Spacek, and Lange's good friend Tuesday Weld (who looked so much like Jessica that the two considered doing a film as sisters). There was no one, apparently, who didn't want the part. "Even those who felt they were too old, or not exactly right, said they understood this woman," Sanger told *The New York Times*. The standard opening line, Sanger said, was "I am Frances Farmer"—"and then they would go into a litany of the horrendous things that had happened in their lives."

Jessica Lange's leg up on this stellar competition was three-fold. First of all, her resemblance to Farmer was uncanny. They came from the same North European stock that had settled the northernmost states—both with high forehead, strong jaw and mouth, deepset eyes, and high cheekbones. Or, as Mel Brooks put it somewhat less delicately, "It's hard to find a beauty with big bones. Frances and Jessica are both Midwesterners with large frames." Second, as a still relatively unknown actress, she didn't carry a high price tag—nor an identity that would overwhelm the part; Mel Brooks was clearly looking for bargains, which was one reason he hired first-time director Clifford. And one final reason, which circulated in Hollywood with no more or less validity than any other rumor, was Lange's steamy outtakes from *The Postman Always Rings Twice*. According to Eric Kasum, a syndicated columnist, Clifford showed co-producer Jonathan Sanger the torrid footage, which convinced Sanger that Lange could handle the role. Kasum went on to report that Hollywood insiders thought the role was "more than the relatively untried actress could handle." Even producer Sanger, in a less-than-confident statement about his leading lady, said that "It may make her or break her, but this film will put Jessica Lange on the map." Mel Brooks was, in fact, more partial to Lange's buddy, Tuesday Weld, who had not had a good leading part in some time.

If Hollywood was waiting for Jessica Lange to fall on her

face, they had come to the wrong woman. Lange, as producer Sanger put it to *The New York Times*, "obviously had more acting training than anybody knew." In the spring of 1981, while still breast-feeding her newborn daughter by Baryshnikov, she worked on each scene with her coach, Sandra Seacat. Seacat had been an important and influential member of the Group Theatre herself, and had expanded her theatrical repertoire in recent years to include techniques from Eastern meditation. Lange regularly used those deep relaxation techniques on the set to improve her concentration in the grueling role.

The emotional preparation was a great deal of work. She went through the script scene by scene, picking the scene apart and then deciding what area in her own life corresponded most closely to the emotions the scene required. Every day in New York City that spring, she brought a nanny to stay with baby Shura for three hours while she worked on the role and went to the gym to trim off the excess ten pounds from her pregnancy. Her sleeping patterns, of course, remained disrupted by the breast-feeding, but she introduced a bottle fairly early to prepare the baby for upcoming separations when principal shooting began in Los Angeles. She began inquiries for the second nanny she would need in Los Angeles. But the baby would be coming with her to the set each day, Lange vowed. "She isn't going to have a conventional upbringing, in a vine-covered cottage," Lange observed. Children, she knew well from her own childhood of perpetual motion, were resilient.

From the Paramount vaults, Lange screened every movie Farmer made—seventeen in all, and each worse than the one before. If Jessica regretted *King Kong*, her experience was nothing compared to what Frances went through. It was tragic, Lange thought as she watched them. Most of those movies should never have been made. Lange memorized which film was being made at which point in the script, including the unfinished *No Escape*, which ended when Farmer struck a hairdresser and broke her jaw. The disintegration of the actress was clear from the films, and the rage they must have engendered in such a talented actress was obvious—but the most helpful bits of celluloid for Jessica were some 8-millimeter home movies that someone had found of Frances doing summer stock in the east in the late thirties. "Watching her walk and move gave me more to work from than any of the films she did," said Lange, always the mime, the student of physical gesture. "It was fascinating."

Naturally, Lange had read the two books about Farmer, every newspaper and magazine interview with Farmer she could get her hands on, and an unpublished autobiography. She talked to Lou Kibbee, a Seattle, Washington, resident who had been working with Farmer on her autobiography at the time of Farmer's death.

In Los Angeles, in the meantime, preproduction on *Frances* moved ferociously ahead, with the producers anxiously following reports in the trades of an impending directors' strike that would stall their film. After eight drafts in two years, Chris Devore and Eric Bergren departed for the latest Dino De Laurentiis extravaganza, *Dune*. Writer Nicholas Kazan was brought in for the final polish and for rewrites during principal photography.

Like so many others on the project, production designer Sylbert felt a special affinity for Frances's story. "I'd always wanted to do a story like this," he told *American Cinematographer* in March of 1983. *Frances*, he said, "is about a girl who

constantly goes back home." For Sylbert, who always looked
at his pictures in terms of music, this meant Frances was a
concerto in an A-B-A-C-A form, like a sonata by Mozart that
always returns to its first theme, he said. "The girl starts at
sixteen and goes to Russia, New York, and Hollywood and
comes back a star. She leaves and goes to Hollywood and New
York and comes home again, a mess. She leaves and goes to a
mental institution and comes home again." The ending, from
a "This Is Your Life" episode, is the coda. For the three major
locales in Farmer's life, Sylbert selected colors in three groups
—browns for the Farmers' home in Seattle, whites for Hollywood and New York (where Farmer starred in *Golden Boy* and
fell in love with Clifford Odets), gray for the mental institution. Sylbert stayed away from bright colors, because acrylic
dyes had not yet been invented in the thirties.

The irony is that while this kind of detail for emotional
accuracy in the sets and costumes was being carried out, the
emotional detail in the actual words was still in a state of
disarray. The problems with this surefire story were starting
to materialize. The character of Harry York became the film's
narrator, drawing a sepia-tinted gauze over what in reality was
Farmer's solitary struggle with alcohol, mental and physical
abuse in hospital wards, and her demonic mother. A rather
sunny girlhood, during which Farmer wrote an essay that
brought her national attention—"God Dies"—was portrayed
with an emphasis on the running battle between parent and
child that Farmer described in her own memoirs. William
Arnold (author of *Shadowland*), seeing the script, insisted that
it was not based on original material.

With Harry York in the picture, rescuing Lange every reel
or so, Farmer seemed to be afflicted with nothing worse than

an inability to stay with a perfectly good man who wanted her. The relationship which defined Farmer's life and downfall, that with her mother, was never developed with the clarity and intensity it required to make sense of Farmer's life. Lange knew that York was "contrived," but there it was. The script was still undergoing rewrites by Nicholas Kazan when Lange herself arrived in Los Angeles. Savoring her last relatively unfettered days with her little daughter, Lange settled into a rented house with the baby, a nanny, and a black unclipped poodle that Misha had given her, named, of all things, Masha. Except for brief vacation time, she would be a full-time working mom for more than a year.

The directors' strike, to everyone's relief, did not materialize, and Lange officially began her life as Frances. Arriving at Paramount studios, the scene of her own unhappy experience in *King Kong*, "was an odd feeling," admitted Lange in a January interview in the *Los Angeles Times*' "Calendar" section, but perhaps a not unfitting introduction to the part—and the parallels. "So much seems to have happened since then," Lange commented in a moment of understatement. "I just hope," she added, "that my work in *Frances* will finally erase the memory of *King Kong*. It should. It's the best woman's part I've ever come across. . . ." That was for damn sure.

With her makeup woman, Dorothy Pearl—by now one of her close friends—and the director of photography Kovacs, who had risen to fame with Nicholson and Rafelson filming *Easy Rider* and *Five Easy Pieces,* Lange sat under glaring lights for eight days of tests, primarily for close-ups and still photographs needed to establish the makeup and lighting for each different period in Farmer's life. The looks required took Lange from age sixteen to age forty, from high-school innocent to Hollywood glamour girl to ravaged mental patient. To hear those involved with that aspect of production makes it clear to what extent the visual details were attended to in the film. It was as if the filmmakers felt that if the set design, the close-ups, the number of angles were correct, the film itself could not go wrong. Frames from these tests, from the film close-ups, were blown up to eight-by-ten stills and put on a big board to be analyzed along with the structure of the film. Sylbert and his crew patiently searched for and meticulously decorated sets that said more about the characters than the dialogue was ever allowed to.

Dottie Pearl realized, with some surprise, that the toughest challenge was not making her friend look fourteen years younger, but trying to turn that creamy skin into a washed-out forty. Kovacs noticed that part of Lange's sense of intense emotion was the simple point that her eyes had a natural quality of watering, so that she always appeared on the verge of tears. He designed his lighting schemes to include eye lights that would take advantage of this. According to Laszlo Kovacs, Hollywood's best technicians were working on this film, "because they feel the movie is important. This was human drama and you see very little of that today."

Lange greeted old friends from her days of *The Postman Always Rings Twice*—Charles Mulvehill, an associate producer on *Frances*, had co-produced the earlier film, for example. Kim Stanley arrived in Los Angeles having dropped fifty pounds, thanks to a liquid protein diet. Jessica was "trepiditious," she admitted, about meeting this great star of Broadway and the London stage from the fifties. At fifty-six, an actress from Frances Farmer's own generation, Stanley had been with the original Group Theatre, had studied acting with Elia Kazan and Lee Strasberg, and had even known the brilliant, egomaniacal playwright Clifford Odets, who turned out to be

Frances Farmer's nemesis. Stanley's own film career was limited to *The Goddess* (1958) and *Seance on a Wet Afternoon* (1964), which earned her an Oscar nomination. William Inge had written *Bus Stop* for her, Paddy Chayevsky *The Goddess*. But in the mid-sixties, Stanley vanished from sight, to emerge only for a 1977 film called *The Three Sisters*, and now for this. Once considered the most gifted actress of her generation, she had been teaching acting at the College of Santa Fe.

But Jessica shouldn't have worried. Stanley and Lange spent two weeks together that summer getting acquainted, swimming together each morning, baking bread, and improvising on Frances and Lillian. Stanley had also researched the Farmer family, talking to Lou Kibbee in Washington as well. The two theorized about mothers and daughters, about powerful parents and the children who yearn to please them with public triumphs. They would finish the film as close friends, eager to work together again in the near future (which they did on the Showtime production of *Cat on a Hot Tin Roof*).

"Kim works exactly the way I like to work," said Lange. "She's very private, nothing is discussed. There's a mystery to the work." The two became a mutual admiration society. Lange, Stanley told *Time* magazine, is "the kind of dame I want to work with—quick, open, smart."

And then there was Sam. With various parallels to Frances Farmer's great love, Clifford Odets, Shepard, at thirty-eight, was considered the most prolific and celebrated playwright of his generation. By 1982, this taciturn writer had penned one hundred plays, had forty of them produced, and won a Pulitzer Prize (in 1979, for *Buried Child*) and ten Obies. His acting career in major features began quietly with a near-silent lead in Terence Malick's elegiac *Days of Heaven* (1978), but had proceeded apace with roles in *Resurrection* and *Raggedy Man*. Though firmly established as one of the major forces in American theater, he had not, however, reached the superstar status that would be his with the part of Chuck Yeager in the 1984 Philip Kaufman film *The Right Stuff*, based on Tom Wolfe's sarcastic look at the American astronaut program. He chose *Frances*, he said, "because it is like a Greek tragedy."

Shepard was a writer whose imagination stabbed viciously through macho dreamscapes. Women were few and far between in the universe of his imagination, though they peopled it actively in his real life. He met Jessica Lange through his subsidiary, though much more visible, career as an actor. Graeme Clifford, the editor who had fallen in love with Jessica's face as he cut celluloid versions of it in *The Postman Always Rings Twice*, cast Shepard in the fictional character of Harry because of what he called Shepard's "enigmatic sexuality" and "because I thought he and Jessica would get along well together."

Another very private person, like Lange, and a charismatic male with a stud reputation to rival Baryshnikov's (during his rock music phase he had cavorted with Patti Smith), he could easily have attended the same downtown parties as Lange in Soho ten years before. They also shared the itinerant upbringing by fathers who switched jobs every two years in obscure towns in the Midwest. Of his co-star, Shepard would only say at the time that she was "an intuitive actress. Every take is different."

Whatever the reason for the rapport, the two were discreet —indeed, how much energy could even Jessica Lange have with fourteen-hour days on the set and a baby under a year old to care for? Though the cast and crew were aware "they were a couple," as one put it, before the shoot was half over, the press never got wind of the affair during production, except for the couple being caught by photographers dining out at a Los Angeles restaurant in January. That event made the gossip columns more for Shepard's violent reaction—flinging his leather coat at one of the photographers—than anything else. Nothing implicating a love affair between the two appeared in print until long after Lange had won her Oscar. Indeed, the involvement seemed like no more than one of the usual brief flings that flare up on the sets of movies like so many fireflies on a summer night—an attraction induced by a film, acted on briefly, and terminated safely. Shepard was, after all, married. He'd always returned to O-lan, his wife of fourteen years and the mother of his then twelve-year-old son, Jesse Mojo. And Lange had Baryshnikov.

What was not quiet was Lange's immersion in her role. She became, for all intents and purposes, Frances Farmer. It was "a nervous breakdown a day," she would tell one reporter. Pure rage, screaming, seething pain and frustration, for twelve, fourteen hours a day were the norm for the next five months. Lange—instinctive, private, determined—rented out a piece of her soul for the part. "What you're seeing on the screen is only one one-thousandth of what was actually expended, with the number of takes and what was cut out," she would say when it was over. "What you're actually seeing on film is one minute of film time that was an entire day of rage." Graeme had seen Lange turn into a sullen, amoral panther for *The Postman Always Rings Twice.* Now he watched as Jessica "went a little crazy on the set." He explained away Lange's combativeness by telling reporters, "Jessie needed to act out a little. She was testing the authorities." But he was insistent about what he wanted. It was "emotionally taxing," even for the technical people, Kovacs told *American Cinematographer*, "because you could never divorce yourself from the intensity in her performance. You were there and you were part of it and it just drained your emotions. Can you imagine what it did to her when she had to do it over and over?"

Lange was in every scene, spanning Seattle, Mexico, Los Angeles, New York. Though she and Graeme were friends, they had screaming matches about the film. Like Vivien Leigh fighting to keep Scarlett O'Hara a human being on the chaotic set of *Gone With the Wind* (one of Lange's favorite films), Jessica Lange battled to keep Frances true-to-life in the midst of what reviewers would later consider an inadequate and sometimes inaccurate script and a director and producer who believed "no one deliberately tried to victimize Frances," as Clifford told *The New York Times*. Producer Sanger was on the set next to Clifford for most of the shoot as well and had gone over "every line of dialogue" in the script. Later, he would eagerly tell the trade press (and, by extension, the rest of the industry) that *Frances* was "not a downer." Lange stayed "tense and angry," as she put it, not just during the long weeks of shooting, but for months afterward.

But the hardest part was what wasn't on the set: her baby daughter. Though Lange raced to the baby's side in her dressing room with the nanny whenever there was a break in the shooting, Shura cried whenever her mother left for another take. "It was really hard to leave her all day," Lange admitted. And Lange herself would come home "overwrought from the intensity of the emotion all day." But on many days, of course, the good-natured baby brought Jessica back to herself from the ravaged woman whose life she was having trouble separating from her own. "It's hard to feel too terrible with one of these around," she said to one interviewer as she tousled the baby's blonde head.

What was it that spoke so strongly to Lange, one wonders, that she would give so much of herself to a role? "All through life I've harbored anger rather than expressed it at the moment," Lange told *Newsweek*. "Once I started on *Frances*, I discovered it was literally a bottomless well."

"It devastated me," Lange admitted after it was all over, "to maintain that for eighteen weeks, to be immersed in this state of rage for twelve to fourteen hours a day. It spilled over into other aspects of my life. I was really hell to be around. I took on the characteristic of Frances that was elemental to her demise—battling every little thing that came along." At certain points in the shoot, she felt certain that "Frances was with us," her spirit watching over the Universal set, where Warren Beatty's office, a former Frances Farmer dressing room, was converted back into its original use for the film.

Though everyone could see the logic of not doing so, the film was shot out of sequence. "Which meant that one day I'd be doing a breakdown scene," Lange complained to the *Los Angeles Times*, "and a month later I'd have to do the scene leading up to it." Lange had urged that the film be shot in sequence, "but no one listened to me." Sanger recognized the problem and chalked it up to the low budget—$8 to $10 million. "It has been hard on Jessica," he admitted. "It's hard to get the level of insanity to match from one scene to the next . . . we can never get any distance because we're moving too fast. We're not able to shut down and catch up."

The set, in fact, became increasingly tense as Clifford's inexperience, at least as far as Lange was concerned, became abundantly clear. Clifford insisted on take after take after take—far too many, according to Lange. Clifford, of course, as a first-time director, felt everything lay on the line for him in this film. Along with that, the Australian, after two decades of editing, had a natural film editor's bias, wanting reams of takes and every conceivable angle with which to play in the editing room. But for Lange, for a part like this, it was an agony. "The set was not well run," Lange told the *Los Angeles Times'* Roderick Mann, "and there was far too much footage shot of everything. There's nothing wrong with overshooting unless it's fairly taxing on the actor. With a film like this, it was."

One scene on the Farmer staircase, a confrontation between mother and daughter, was shot "twenty or thirty times," Lange said. In this pivotal fight, takes were being made from so many angles and directions that "to get that pitch was difficult . . . [Clifford] broke it up and we started in the middle. We didn't have that run in, that natural build. We did it over and over and we were both so exhausted." Finally, Stanley took Jessica's hand in hers and suggested to her young friend: "Let's just start from the very beginning." It was one of the few times that Kim Stanley offered suggestions on the set, and it turned the scene around. "From that point on, it had all the electricity that it was supposed to have," Lange said.

Many scenes brought Lange to abrupt confrontations with her own inner demons, sometimes with emotions she'd never confronted before. The insulin-shock scenes, showing an early form of shock treatment to induce convulsions, felt every bit as humiliating to Jessica as an actress, lying prone under a white sheet, as she imagined they did to her real-life counterpart suffering the actual physical results.

Or the memorable scene when Frances stops on the stairs, in her parents' home in Seattle, and tells her parents that she doesn't love them. Lange wanted to play that scene as a statement of emotional independence, as something victorious. But she changed her approach to the one used in the film, a wrenching moment where her voice breaks with hurt, as she admonishes her parents not to think she loves them anymore "because I don't . . . I can't." In the end she switched approaches, "because, in fact, Frances never was a victor over her mother. She never was victorious." Pause for Miss Lange, for whom defeat did not sit easily: "That was really a tough one to play."

Frustrations could be as simple as a prop door that didn't work. In a wrenching scene, much of it shot from overhead, Farmer is accosted by policemen breaking into the Knickerbocker Hotel in the middle of the night. Farmer, drunk, naked, is roused from sleep by pounding on the door and the jangling ring of the phone. She grabs a sheet as she races to the bathroom and kneels, cowering, in a corner, waiting for the police to break in and haul her away. In one of the film's few nude scenes, Lange commenced screaming in one corner of the bathroom—and the bathroom door stuck. The actors playing cops on the other side couldn't get it open. They played the scene again and the door stuck again. When this happened for the fourth time, Lange hit the roof. Couldn't they at least have checked to make sure the damn door opened before she shed her clothing and got into character? The entire scene, lasting no more than three minutes of film time, took four days to shoot. Lange was disgusted. She began to feel as used, abused, and manipulated as Frances herself.

Reports began to circulate, as reports do in Hollywood, that Jessica was "difficult." Lange responded to Gene Shalit on the

"Today" show, who asked, when it was all over, if she had, indeed, been "difficult"—and just what that word meant. "I don't know," answered a smiling Lange, all somber responsibility in a dark jacket, black scarf, and white shirt. "I don't know for sure. I fought for things real hard that I thought were right, that I still think are right, that are in the film and make it a better film.

"I didn't want them to take the edge off of it—I didn't want them to take the edge off of her," Lange explained. Later that year, working with Dustin Hoffman, who similarly locked horns with his director, Sydney Pollack, on the set of *Tootsie*, Lange saw the same phenomenon. "When a whole movie kind of rests on your back and you know you're up there all the time on screen and you're either going to make it or break it, that pressure makes you fight. I mean—I fought like a dog for things I believed in. Maybe that's what they mean—I didn't say, 'Okay, I'll do it your way.' If I thought it was wrong, I wouldn't do it." Period.

As if the fictional turmoil Lange lived with weren't enough, her husband, thirty-seven-year-old Paco Grande, a filmmaker she had met as a student in Minnesota and married in 1970, filed a highly publicized divorce in New York City. Grande had lost much of his eyesight to a degenerative eye disease. Now disabled, he was suing for support and a Manhattan Supreme Court judge agreed. A temporary order in February 1982 required Lange to pay $300 a week, retroactive to October 1981—a sum totalling $5,700, along with $2,500 of Grande's legal fees. The final decision required hefty monthly payments which have not been made public, but which Lange said are "a lot." Grande, who filed his suit in the closing days of 1981, had asked for $2,000 to $3,000 a month.

* * *

31

At Christmastime, Lange arrived with Shura in tow for their first Christmas in her new log cabin in the woods near Holyoke, Minnesota. The toll the film was taking on Jess physically—sunken cheeks, dark circles under her eyes—shocked her parents. "I looked terrible," Lange said ruefully. The quiet, as always in the northern woods, was palpable. Misha Baryshnikov had not joined her, but family huddled around, including her beloved grandparents—all more worried than impressed by Jessica's latest adventure in Hollywood. Shura toddled on the rugs on the wood floor with her cousins. Jessica curled up in front of the crackling fire with a massive recent biography of Clifford Odets, where she read, among other things, that Fay Wray, the original *King Kong* girl, had been an avid follower of the Group Theatre in the thirties—and one of Odet's many loves.

Lange and Shura returned to Los Angeles in January for six more weeks of shooting. Courtroom scenes, where a gray-suited Farmer is led before judges and then to jail, took place in an old San Pedro courthouse and contained some of Lange's best moments in the film. "Profession?" asks the policeman after she's been dragged in. "Cocksucker," retorts Lange, and then gives him a "What's the matter with you, big boy?" look that sums up Farmer's defiance in a single moment.

One of the most difficult scenes for Lange required no violence at all. Frances Farmer, according to the film, and as strongly suggested by her biographer, Arnold, was used at Steilacom, the mental institution, to demonstrate a new, quick procedure for lobotomy. The lobotomy sequence itself appeared frightening, but for Lange consisted mostly of lying on her back with a lot of makeup making her appear bruised and stunned. But the final scene of the film brought the reality home. Lange had to play the ultimate defeat of her heroine as a dulled, post-lobotomy Frances Farmer on a 1958 episode of "This Is Your Life."

In 1958, Sam Shepard, then just a kid, stared at the flickering television set from an Army base and saw this episode, probably one of the saddest in that series' history. ("They took away her life and then gave her an Edsel," he quipped.) Farmer, vague and blank in a black dress, is given a new car after answering such questions as: "Were you ever an alcoholic?" and "Did you ever take dope?" The producers managed to get a copy of the original show. When Lange saw it for the first time, she burst into tears. "I was so overwhelmed, so moved," she said.

From then on, Lange studied the tape obsessively. The episode "loomed in front of me like an insurmountable problem," she told Shalit. She memorized every gesture, every inflection: "There were a million things going on in her face, in her eyes." Speaking of eyes, Kovacs decided that the best way to show a lobotimized Frances was to take out the eye lights he'd been using the entire film. The scene finally fell into place. Jessica Lange, as a lobotimized Frances Farmer, is terrifyingly flat, slowed in her movements, like a walking corpse.

After the film's release, when Clifford's directorial debut went virtually ignored in the torrent of praise for Lange's performance, the two conducted a brief feud in the pages of the *Los Angeles Times'* "Calendar" section. Clifford commented that Lange hadn't had to "act" for the role in *Frances:* "She just let out all the stuff she usually represses." Lange read this and got on the phone instantly for a very unrepressed rebuttal.

Far from being easy or natural, Lange insisted, *"Frances* was the hardest stretch I've ever done." She listed in public the complaints about overshooting and the badly run set. The controversy eventually settled down, with Clifford modifying his statement in yet another article. But even so, no one stepped back to analyze how a film with an actress so good could turn out to be so bad. Lange did tell the "Calendar" writer that she was hurt by the reviews, that she felt they were unfair.

But both she and Stanley understood full well why the movie had failed. The two aspects of filmmaking that are most easily tampered with—the writing and the editing—both were subject to the doubts, ultimately, about showing Frances Farmer's life as the pit of despair it really was. Precisely the elements that had attracted Marie Yates, Graeme Clifford, writers like Arnold or Rex Reed, Jessica herself, to this tragic heroine—her solitary refusal to aquiesce, her ferocious anger, her paradigmatic lock with a powerful parent that afflicts so many creative people—precisely these elements were jettisoned, in the final analysis, by producers and Universal studio executives terrified of releasing something perceived as a "downer."

A computer-selected audience of 450 in Washington, D.C., found the original length of two hours and twenty minutes too long. A third of the audience walked out during a violent rape sequence which was cut in the final version—the rape of Farmer at the mental ward, a constant theme in her autobiography. Scenes which made more sense of Farmer's breakdown and her relationship with her mother were dropped in favor of keeping the romance with Harry York intact. Said an angry Kim Stanley to the *Hollywood Reporter* several months later: "I'm not mad at Graeme Clifford. I'm damn mad at the studio that thinks that the American public can sit still for five hours of football but can't sit still for an emotional study of a grown woman." The result of the editing, Stanley said, was "constant coitus interruptus."

Months later, after *Tootsie* was finished shooting, when Lange had wowed the critics and awaited her Oscar nominations, she would stop, suddenly, and find herself "on the verge of tears, overwhelmed with sadness" about *Frances*. "Roles," she concluded, "are baggage that you carry around." Even three years later, when interviewed by *New York Times* reporter Dena Kleiman, Lange made it clear: "I'll never do a role like that again."

3

TOOTSIE

Tootsie was a landmark movie in many ways. For the first time in recent memory, a leading male actor, Dustin Hoffman, played a woman for the majority of the film. He got $4 million from Columbia Pictures to do it. He had more power on the set than any nonproducing actor had ever commanded. The movie grossed more than $140 million and became one of the highest-grossing films in Columbia Pictures' history. But for our purposes, one landmark outshines all of these. *Tootsie* is the movie in which America fell in love with Jessica Lange.

They saw her through the eyes of Michael Dorsey, a hapless deceptor who had donned the trappings of the opposite sex in order to get work as an actor. Cast as a woman in a soap opera, he falls in love with the soap-opera star, Julie Nichols, who is herself the girlfriend of the soap's director, played by Dabney Coleman. Like Lange, the character was unmarried, with a fourteen-month-old baby (played by Amy Lawrence) and a family still on the farm. In the course of the film, Julie turns to Dorothy for support and advice, even as Michael falls ever more in love with her—until Julie suspects Dorothy of being a lesbian and, finally, learns the truth and accepts Dorothy as Michael, albeit reluctantly, in the film's final moments.

Jessica played the soap opera star as someone who is, as Lange said, "pixielated"—not dumb, but understandably confused as a real woman by the same things that were confusing Dustin's character as a fake one. In point of fact, Lange did appear to be the real Tootsie of the film's title, a kind of vulnerable, sweet, inadvertently gorgeous and helpless creature, played so effortlessly, apparently, and so naturally that she corresponded exactly to the kind of guileless, down-home innocence that yuppie men dream about as they stare across the conference room table at women in steel-gray business suits.

When people say—as they invariably do—"Oh, Jessica Lange? I really like her, she's great," they are talking about the character in *Tootsie*, which is where several million people saw Lange for the first and only time. Her appeal was not haphazard, according to Susan Dworkin in *Making Tootsie* (Newmarket Press, 1983). Director Sydney Pollack had remembered Lange's ready sensuality from *King Kong*. He needed a leading lady whose appeal to his Michael Dorsey-cum-Dorothy Michaels would need no explanations and take very little screen time, and Lange qualified. She also qualified on another count—after hiring Hoffman at $4 million (and 3 percent of the gross, which eventually worked out to some $20 million more), producer Pollack couldn't afford another superstar salary. Lange, post-*Postman* and post-*Frances*, but pre-Academy Awards, was still a bargain. (Co-producer Dick Richards, an original owner of the property but not involved in the actual production, also knew Lange from her days as a model in Manhattan.)

Much of what this film tried to say about femininity had to be said by the character of Julie Nichols, which is another reason Pollack wanted her in the part. So Lange was given a cuddly baby and dressed and surrounded in soft colors and soft fabrics—beiges and pinks, suedes and sweatpants. Her voice is airy, lilting, hesitant. She guzzles white wine and snuggles Amy and is terrified of the babysitter. All the things that made her so instantly appealing to Hoffman made her instantly appealing to the audience, as well.

Little did the audiences lining up for *Tootsie* that Christmas realize how little Lange herself identified with the part. The moviegoing public identified Lange with the character of Julie Nichols—winning, eager, unself-conscious, charming—but Lange herself did not. "When I did *Tootsie,*" Lange told *Vanity Fair*'s John Heilpern, "I never read a review. Sometimes I don't even remember doing it. But with *Frances,* I read everything. I identified with everything. And ultimately, all the recognition came from *Tootsie.* I couldn't believe it." In the thousands of remarks Lange made in the months preceding the Academy Awards, a scant handful were for *Tootsie,* and these were only in the context of comparing the Julie Nichols character with her beloved Frances. "Tootsie is a real easygoing, modern girl," said Lange (referring to her character as Tootsie). "So I don't feel the connection with the character in *Tootsie* like I do with Frances." The two characters, she said, "aren't really comparable." Of the onscreen persona, one resident of the *Tootsie* set observed drily, "She can be as charming as that—when she wants to be." And yet, to old friends in her hometown of Cloquet, Minnesota, *Tootsie* was the first movie where they recognized their Jessie. "I saw *Tootsie* and I thought: That's Jess," said one high-school buddy.

Jessica, by this point an established actress, if not yet a superstar, brought to the set her friend Dorothy Pearl for her makeup and Toni Walker for her hair. Mira Rostoya, the famous acting coach of Montgomery Clift, was on the set with her throughout the shoot, just as Seacat had been for *Frances.*

As she did with the *Frances* shoot, Lange brought Shura and her nanny to the dressing room whenever possible. Baby toys cluttered the dressing room, and during the long battles that ensued between Pollack and Hoffman, Lange would retire to the room and play with Shura.

For all the sunniness of the part, the film itself was, once again, not an easy shoot. Jessica Lange had no vacation to speak of—merely three weeks between the closing of *Frances* and the start-up of *Tootsie* in which to move herself and her baby back to New York. Sam Shepard was on his way to San Francisco to play the role of Chuck Yeager in *The Right Stuff*, the role that would earn him superstar status and an Oscar nomination, and Lange went uncertainly to reunite with her baby's father, Misha Baryshnikov, who was himself a little fed up with the aspects of Frances's character that had been dominating Jessica's personality for so many months.

It was the drain of the *Frances* role, in fact, which led to her taking the *Tootsie* part in the first place. Lange was sent the script while in the middle of shooting *Frances,* and very nearly turned the producers down.

"I almost said no to *Tootsie* because I just couldn't imagine having the energy after doing *Frances*," said Jessica in Los Angeles early in December of 1982, the month in which her entire career would take a quantum leap into stratospheric stardom. "But at the same time, I thought I really needed something. And Kim Stanley said do a comedy as soon as you can just to get your mind off it." Kim Stanley, playing Jessica Lange's onscreen mother, assumed some maternal authority offscreen as well. Jessica said yes.

The film was shot entirely in New York, which was an advantage for her home life, but it lasted sixteen weeks, beginning in March and closing in sweltering July heat, when Jessica and Dustin Hoffman played the film's closing scene on a 90-degree New York sidewalk. "I'm telling you, I get these long ones," she said ruefully. The *Tootsie* set offered plenty of heat on its own. "Dustin Hoffman and Sydney Pollack had huge differences in concept on how they wanted things done," said Owen Roizman, the stoic and reliable director of photography, in *American Cinematographer.* "Day in and day out there were problems. Some days went smoothly, but most days didn't." Hoffman, of course, was such a big star that he and Pollack were more or less co-equal in the task of interpreting the title character's traits. Teri Garr, readying to do her famous shrieking scene, noted that "by that point in the shooting, Dustin Hoffman had Sydney so beaten that we could do anything." Actually, Pollack established a policy of letting the actors get "freebies"—their own takes done their own way— at the end of each scene, and some of the film's most comic moments generated from that freedom.

After her own months of confrontation on the set of *Frances,* Lange carefully absented herself from the heated aesthetic debates of Pollack and Hoffman. It was, for all its drawbacks, "a fun shoot," according to one good friend. And Lange understood the situation. For one thing, chameleonlike, she apparently became as cheerful and charming as her character was intended to be, according to Julia Cameron in a cover story on Lange in *American Film.* No more reports of "difficulties" on this set. For Lange, the tension was off. It was a relief to be playing a supporting part, and not shouldering the entire responsibility of a film, as in *Frances.* And she respected Hoffman enormously. "Dustin was just extraordinary," she said. "His tenacity and endurance are quite stunning and I really admire him for it."

But there were problems acting with him. At the beginning,

particularly, the heavy makeup Hoffman wore as Dorothy fell apart after a few hours under the lights, and everyone would stand, bored and tense, waiting while the problem was corrected. Dorothy Pearl began to get involved in Hoffman's complex makeup problems when she arrived on the set, after three makeup specialists had already been brought in to deal with his heavy beard, wrinkles, and other problems. She was such a help that the makeup staff wanted to use her on Hoffman full-time, but Lange refused to relinquish Pearl's services, and a third person was hired.

Lange was so beautiful that keeping Hoffman a convincing woman under the same lights as Lange was difficult. "The only real problem I had on *Tootsie* was that Dustin Hoffman wanted to look as good as Jessica Lange," laughed Owen Roizman. "Magic is my hobby, but it's not my livelihood! Jessica, of course, was really easy to light. . . ."

Makeup problems or no, Hoffman was so convincing as Dorothy Michaels that Lange said, "When someone asked me if I found it distracting playing opposite someone in drag, I said it had never occurred to me that he was in drag. He actually became that woman." The two of them worked spontaneously, in the nature of the entire production, on bits of business to add to the comic routines. The only problem was that Dustin was a talker. "That was the only area that was difficult for me because I don't like verbalizing things," Lange said. For the same reason, Sydney Pollack found Lange hard to direct—in a way that was different from the way his determined and obsessive star, Hoffman, was difficult. "Nothing comes out literally with Jessica," Pollack told *The Daily News*. "Sometimes with actors, you get exactly what you put in. You give them a direction and they do just what you tell them." With Lange, however, Pollack would give her a direction and

"it would always come out slightly different from the input."
"It's like a gyroscope that you push forward and it moves to the right," he said. From reading articles about Jessica—not from talking to Lange herself—Pollack discovered that his leading lady had studied painting, and the problem fell into place. "You can feel that she's an artist," he said. "There's always a little more going on than expected."

Echoing an oft-stated opinion of anyone who's worked with her, Pollack told *The Daily News* that "She's an extremely private person. In Hollywood, when you're making a movie, everyone goes through this ritual of instant intimacy, which is of course highly suspect. But Jessica doesn't allow that kind of intimacy. I like her and I would work with her again," Pollack concluded, "but I still don't feel I really know her."

For all its problems, Kim Stanley had been right on the money about *Tootsie* as therapy after *Frances. Tootsie* "really eased me back into real life, got me away from the character of Frances, which was just murdering me," Lange told *Newsweek*. Baryshnikov took time off from directing the upcoming season at the American Ballet Theater and watched the shooting on a few occasions, including that last scene on the New York street. The film, which took four years of Dustin Hoffman's and Sydney Pollack's lives, took a comparatively short four months of Jessica Lange's—and established her as a major star. Ironically, the sweat and effort of creating *Frances* could not bring her the fame brought by the far simpler work—on her part—in *Tootsie.* In the end, it was her cheerful blonde soap-star role that won an Oscar—not Dustin Hoffman for *Tootsie,* not herself for *Frances*—but for the daffy girl whose best girlfriend turns out to be a man.

4

THE CHAPTER CALLED FAME

T he double billing is what made Jessica Lange. It was a masterstroke. For one thing, *Tootsie* became the only unqualified commercial and critical success that Jessica Lange has been involved in to date. It became, in fact, one of the best-selling comedies in the history of the business. But, more importantly, it balanced *Frances*. It was as if *Frances* were the Ph.D. and *Tootsie* were the wedding—the one validated her as an actress among actresses, the other as a honey among honeys. To have both performances flickering out at New York audiences within a week of each other in the last few weeks of 1982 did something grim, serious portrayals alone couldn't seem to do: People, in one giant fell swoop of amnesia, forgot *King Kong* even existed. Jessica Lange was finally Jessica Lange.

"I have never," declared her former lover, Bob Fosse, "seen someone go from so cold to so hot." While *Frances* opened on December 3 in New York, *Tootsie* followed on December 10 in New York City and Los Angeles, in time to qualify for the Oscars. On December 17, *Frances* opened in more cities, and on December 19, *Tootsie* opened in more than a thousand theaters across the country. While *Frances*'s box office was disappointing, and *Tootsie*'s great—belying the bad word-of-mouth this film had gotten from its tempestuous, overbudget shoot—praise for Lange was unanimous on both counts.

"Magnificent," wrote *The New York Times'* Vincent Canby of her in *Frances*. "Here is a performance so unfaltering, so tough, so intelligent, and so humane that, it seems as if Miss Lange is just now, at long last, making her motion picture debut." Carrie Rickey in the *Village Voice* wrote: "Lange has a rare intelligence and intensity that beam through the piles of bullshit the filmmakers pile before her. . . . Lange . . . is getting a reputation as a girl who buoys along a leaden scenario with considerable skill." Rarely has an actress so risen above her film. "In spite of the film's very real faults in structure and style," wrote Canby in *The New York Times*, "Miss Lange is consistently splendid. She's as fine as the stubborn, sharp-minded teenage girl as she is as the grotesquely misunderstood and frightened woman."

Her reviews for *Tootsie* were equally enthusiastic—"Miss Lange is a total delight," wrote Canby—and the impact of this dual triumph left critics scrambling for adjectives. "In a jolting turnabout that finally has critics throwing kisses instead of hisses, Jessica Lange, 33, has hit Hollywood with a double-whammy the likes of which it hasn't seen in years," gushed *People* magazine. That winter, only Meryl Streep's masterful performance in *Sophie's Choice* was mentioned in the same sentences with Jessica Lange. Not Misha, certainly not *King Kong*. "What both roles confirm," wrote *Newsweek*, "is not only Lange's astonishing range (what's soft and compliant in *Tootsie* is aggressive, almost feral, in *Frances*) but also her magical rapport with the audience. An actress like Meryl Streep might have more sophisticated technique. But her virtuosity keeps you at arm's length. Lange, in contrast, creates instant sympathy." "As a comeback," concluded the *Washington Post*, "it might rank with Rocky Balboa's. . . ."

Whew. After a decade of struggle, Lange, at thirty-three, appeared to have arrived. And yet, at first, Jess appeared to keep herself rather quietly out of the picture of all this attention. Her personal life had done an about-face as she privately grappled with leaving Baryshnikov, her lover of six years and the father of her child, for her new passion, Sam Shepard. She appeared to detach herself from the reviews and the uproar, going so far as to tell one reporter she had no plans to hire a publicist for the upcoming Oscar season. She mentioned to another interviewer that she might just retire to Taos and start painting. She spent much of the fall in Minnesota with her family. She finally had some unfettered time for the baby, now twenty-one months old and already walking and talking—not at all like her mother, a late bloomer who didn't speak until she was three. Lange also felt that she still hadn't recovered fully from the rigors of *Frances*.

In the early weeks of December, as the praise started tumbling in, Lange returned to Los Angeles from film-opening duties in New York, didn't go out, didn't see anyone. But the imperatives of publicity loomed near. "I won't let *Frances* die," she told a reporter. "I have a commitment to *Frances*. I hope it just takes off by itself, but if need be, I will do publicity because I want people to see it." That, however, was just before the "double whammy" opened up—to be nominated for both best actress and best supporting actress, something that hadn't been done since Teresa Wright managed it in 1942. By the time Lange traipsed into Sardi's on the arm of old *King Kong* friend Charles Grodin to pick up the New York Film Critics award for Best Supporting Actress, lying low just wasn't in the cards. Jessica Lange was about to become a household word. She was, in Hollywood's most cherished accolade, hot.

This meant, among other things, that her agent at ICM, Lou Pitt, got every script with a major female role as hers for the picking. With the superstar competition like Jane Fonda and Diane Keaton closing in on forty, Lange was in a class by herself—especially since her colleague, Miss Streep, was pregnant with her second child.

Misha spent Christmas in rehearsals in New York, while the green and white gate on the 120-acre spread opened for Jessica and Shura to spend their second holiday season in the log cabin. Shura, by now, looked like "an apple-cheeked gnome," Jessica said. The Lange relatives, of course, and the old friends "weren't into being overwhelmed," she told reporters, by the sudden presence of a superstar in their midst. Christmas was still Christmas, with siblings and their kids, cousins, second cousins, aunts, uncles, and, of course, her grandparents, hearty and hale in their nineties.

In the year-end wrap-ups about 1982's films, Lange was in much less familiar, but equally welcome, company: The *Los Angeles Times* ran a long article comparing her performance in *Frances* and Ben Kingsley's in *Gandhi*. A *Time* magazine essay constrasted Lange's Frances and Meryl Streep's Sophie from *Sophie's Choice*. For *The New York Times*, "the only comparable triumph . . . is Sophia Loren's in 1961 when she suddenly burst onto our consciousness in *Two Women*."

Duty called. In January, Graeme Clifford had found it a good joke to plan a benefit premiere at the very theater in Seattle, Washington, where Frances Farmer had premiered in *Come and Get It*, and where the sequences of the episode had been shot. It was for a good cause of some kind or other, and a bemused Jessica and Kim Stanley followed along. Jessica half expected the same actress to come out and hand her the keys to the city, just like in the film. "I couldn't resist it!" grinned Clifford.

By the time 1983 had rolled around, it became clear that

Lange would indeed be nominated for Best Supporting Actress for the role in *Tootsie*, and Best Actress for *Frances*. Lange roused herself from her anti-publicity stance and hired a publicist, Mike Myslansky, to campaign for the Oscars. Though Columbia Pictures wanted to stage a multimillion-dollar campaign for her part in *Tootsie*, Lange wanted to concentrate on the top honor, willingly relinquishing campaigning for Best Supporting Actress to her *Tootsie* co-star, Teri Garr, also a nominee.

The interviews were incessant—cover stories in *Rolling Stone*, *American Film*, the *Washington Post*'s "Style" section, lengthy profiles in *Newsweek* and *People*. By the time the final voting week rolled around, all of the Academy could see Lange in a series of appearances on the "Today" show. There, the supposedly reticent Lange talked about Baryshnikov, single motherhood, and the emotional drain of *Frances*.

Lange, not so very private when the occasion warranted otherwise, invited *Life* magazine to her land in Minnesota, where she slung her arms around her dad, Albert, in his coveralls for the camera and cavorted with her baby through fog-filtered sunlight. Meanwhile, the gossip columns buzzed with more important questions, such as: Who would escort Miss Lange to the Academy Awards? Would it be (gasp) Misha? In the end, Jessica showed up in a bright aqua dress on the arm of her younger and only brother George. The "impalation," as *Variety* has accurately dubbed the practice of showing the heads of all the nominees as they wait to hear the envelope's message, showed her delighted with the Oscar for Best Supporting Actress and stoic in the expected loss to Meryl Streep for Best Actress. It was not the top honor that she'd worked so hard for, but it was definitely the little gold man himself in those long fingers. Jessica didn't complain.

Amazingly, no one breathed a word of her affair with Shepard. She kept Misha's status vague, and his reputation, as always, enhanced hers. "Misha and I are not separated," she told *Life* magazine. "We spend an awful lot of time apart because of what we do, but nothing really changes." They spent some of December together in New York—strolling in the Village, watching HBO—before Baryshnikov left on another tour. Little Alexandra watched the American Ballet Theater's rehearsals, while her parents discussed Suzuki violin lessons that Jessica, who'd never mastered an instrument, wanted for Shura, and Misha, who'd mastered three, thought premature. (Shura would be three in March.) Then they parted ways as they had a hundred times before, with one difference: This would be the last.

Jessica and daughter headed back to Los Angeles, where Jessica settled back for the by-now-familiar ritual of telling reporters her life story. Even Misha gallantly consented to the occasional interview for featured stories in *Newsweek* and *Rolling Stone*. In *Rolling Stone*, true enough, he was not exactly kind. "I think she's been in this Frances Farmer role a little too long," he noted to reporter David Rosenthal. Was it true she was ambivalent about ambition, as she claimed in the *Rolling Stone* interview? "It's bullshit," Misha said. "She won't listen to anybody anyway, she'll do what she wants to do."

And she did. She and Sam had been to Holyoke to visit the land in its bleak March beauty. Once the Oscars were over, the two became somewhat open about their affair; by May, their romance made the gossip items. Lange went to look for land in New Mexico. "I certainly don't want to bring up my child in Los Angeles or New York," Lange told Roderick Mann of the *Los Angeles Times*.

That February, Sam Shepard's new play *Fool for Love*

premiered. It was his first play to feature a woman as an equal to the male dramatic leads, in the form of a half-sister who battles interminably with her brother/lover. While the two debate the history of their relationship, a mysterious countess arrives offstage in a limousine. She's been "following him around," the brother says. The sister angrily accuses her lover of sleeping with the countess. Many Shepard friends assumed the play was an examination of his now-concluded marriage with O-lan—the half-sister—and his fledgling affair with Lange.

Shepard, it appeared, had met his match in Lange. He was clearly a man, if not a fool, in love, observed *American Film* reporter Blanche McCrary Boyd, who interviewed him in New Mexico that summer, where Shepard made sure he was interviewed in the same restaurant he knew Lange would be eating at that day. He was, he told his friend Wim Wenders, ready to look at relationships between men and woman at this point in his career. And yet, he told one reporter, he still believed that love between the two sexes could be summarized in two words: "terrible and impossible."

The reaction to Sam Shepard's involvement with Lange brought an incredulous reaction from former peers. It was really too much: "He's the best playwright in America," one friend told *Vanity Fair*'s John Heilpern. "He's a Pulitzer. He's good-looking. He's a movie star. He lives with Jessica Lange. I hate him." That about summed it up. There was no justice.

While Academy Awards hoopla and superstar lovers flurried around her, Lange, according to a hometown friend, was far more concerned about maintaining some semblance of a normal family life, having more children, and protecting her daughter from the obvious ravages of superstar parents. "I think of easing out of acting a few years down the road," Lange told *Newsweek*. "I do know I want a big family. If I could do it without marriage, that would be even better." One of her closest friends in Cloquet was surprised to learn that this new boyfriend down in Santa Fe was a Pulitzer Prize-winning playwright. "She just said she met this guy and something clicked," her high-school friend recalled. It may, perhaps, be only a coincidence that Lange turned to Shepard on the eve of his becoming the "new Gary Cooper," as one paper called him, while Baryshnikov wasn't the icon he once was. The world's reigning dancer, whose power and charisma had made him so appealing to Jessica as an aspiring actress seven years before, was still at the top of his profession but had gradually lost his Boy Wonder status under the stress of directing the American Ballet Theater. A knee injury kept him off the dance floor for five months in 1982. His directorship of the ABT was coming under attack as too "Russified" and ticket sales had dropped with each succeeding year since he took the job in 1980.

One thing was certain, image or no image, there appeared to be little chance of a normal domestic life with the director of one of America's two major dance companies. Touring was the name of the game; invidious backfighting, injuries, temperamental ballerinas, all demanded Baryshnikov's time and energy. Indeed, for all his reputation as a ladykiller, Baryshnikov's only real rival to Jessica Lange were not dancers, but dance—and the ego that sustains the kind of artist that came along only once or twice in a century. Now that the fantasies were coming in fast and thick, Jessica wanted to fulfill a few long-standing ones of her own, ones that her sisters and friends in Minnesota achieved by effortlessly living ordinary lives: a home, a garden, kids. "Sooner or later," Lange told *Newsweek*, "you want to settle down in one place, you get tired of living in sublets." Even Baryshnikov couldn't direct the American Ballet Theater from New Mexico.

Misha visited the set of *Tootsie* at least twice, but he wasn't at the Academy Awards. In the end, observers say, it appears that Lange left him, rather than the breakup being a mutual leave-taking. Said one follower of the New York ballet scene, "He wasn't the same after she left. It just seemed like he wasn't as happy anymore." Little Alexandra is "the light of his life," one friend told the *New York Post*.

Having never been married, there was no stipulation for divorce or custody. Jessica had always taken, it appeared, full responsibility for the child's existence anyway (though Shura bears her father's surname). By spring of 1983, baby Shura and Mom had gone from the cabin in Holyoke, Minnesota, down to Santa Fe. When Sam Shepard came down to supervise the opening of *Fool for Love,* he moved into the house in Hondo Hills. The two rode horses—Shepard indulged in polo—raised Shura, and became the quintessential movie-star couple, an updated Clark Gable-Carole Lombard or, perhaps, Arthur Miller and Marilyn Monroe. And, together, they began scouting the Midwest for the project that they, the hottest couple in the country, were going to make: a movie about farmers.

5

SWEET DREAMS

While Jessica Lange and Sam Shepard whiled away their days on the ranch in New Mexico, the rest of the country drooled. "I think they're the coolest couple in America," one friend gushed. And another change, less overt but equally affecting, permeated Lange's life. She was, truly, a celebrity, once defined by a pundit as someone who is known by people he is glad he doesn't know. That spring of 1983, in articles on completely unrelated subjects—hair salons, baby carriers—Jessica Lange's name would suddenly pop up. The fact that Jessica Lange used so-and-so gave it a seal of authenticity, of a draw to the famous. For the first time in her life, she was recognized wherever she went. Photographers hounded her at openings. Magazines begged her for interviews. In Hollywood, executives who had scoffed at her a few years before now tried to get her on the phone for projects they knew she was perfect for.

But, curiously, at the peak of this appeal, Jessica Lange was not particularly eager to dive into more work. She had her accountant check on how it might be arranged for her to live off the investments of her income. In the press, she claimed she didn't want to be a leading lady after all. "At this point," she

told *The Daily News*, "I would prefer to be known as a character actress. To be a leading lady seems somehow limiting." She
had a point. In the thirties and forties, Lange noted, leading
ladies had delightfully complex roles, but their contemporary
counterparts had been diluted with the passage of time. "I can't
tell you how many scripts I've gotten where the main woman
character is a photographer or a journalist," she complained.
She was also, she added, "making it a point to stay away from
Hollywood. That's been my policy in good times and bad
times. It helps me to hold on to my sanity." Columnist Liz
Smith commented wryly, "Hollywood's hottest actress doesn't
even live in Hollywood."

Two of the parts Lange turned down were not, however,
journalists or photographers, and they weren't to be filmed in
Hollywood. Lange was offered the lead in both *The River*, to
be directed by Mark Rydell *(On Golden Pond)*, which had a
family battling an out-of-control river in Louisiana, and *Places
in the Heart*, directed by Robert Benton *(Kramer vs. Kramer)*
and written by Horton Foote, in which a valiant widow struggles to keep her farm during the Depression.

Lange turned down these parts, not necessarily because
they, too, were limiting, but because she had her own farm
story to tell. Now, whether these subjects influenced her orien-
tation for her next project or not was a subject of some muffled
debate. Lange said that she had found herself drawn to the idea
of producing and acting in her own movie about the perils of
rural life long before she'd been approached for these projects.

To be specific, it was the morning Lange picked up her *Los
Angeles Times* and saw a photograph of an Ohio family whose
farm had been foreclosed that she got the idea for a movie about
the plight of contemporary farmers. "And, of course, the very

next morning, I woke up, thinking it was a real dumb idea!" she admitted. "Nobody was going to be interested. But somebody was interested and then somebody else. And then a studio was going to give me half a million to develop the idea. Then somebody was going to give me $10 million to make the movie." By March of 1983, Lange had contacted the director Hal Ashby (a onetime possibility to direct *Tootsie*, and the Academy Award-nominated director of *Coming Home*) to direct. She also contacted William Wittliff, the successful Texas screenwriter whose credits included *Barbarosa*, *The Black Stallion*, *Honeysuckle Rose*, and *Raggedy Man* (in which Shepard had co-starred), to write a script. Wittliff, who had also produced the latter two films, signed on as co-producer for this one as well. He, Ashby, and Lange made their first trek through the Midwest for possible locations before the Academy Awards in April. And Sam Shepard agreed to take the male lead "because of her," he told *American Film*'s Blanche McCrary Boyd. "We had just gotten together and she was all committed to this thing."

Many in the industry would marvel that Lange would turn her back on Hollywood's hottest roles at the height of her career in order to make her own film (Sissy Spacek would take the part in *The River*, and Sally Field would star in *Places in the Heart* and displace Lange for the 1984 Best Actress Oscar). But such a project was a kind of benchmark for Lange, an official seal of superstar status. Only untouchably hot actors can get away with making political films, can attempt to justify the ethical emptiness of Hollywood success with an image they believe in. Commenting on Frances Farmer's political activities in an interview, Sam Shepard had said with a shrug the year before, "Are any stars really sincere in their politics? It comes from despair over the menialness of film. Being an actress creates desperation."

At any rate, the film was a sign of what a Midwesterner this superstar remained, that she could be moved by the singularly unpopular issue of the depressed farm economy. Anyone close to the rural Midwest in the eighties, as Jessica was through her relatives in Cloquet, had heard, firsthand, of good farmers, third and fourth generation, losing their land, and the tragedies that followed. The situation appeared to Lange to be akin to a contemporary *The Grapes of Wrath* and cried out to be made into a film. It seemed that the media masters of either coast could not hear the screams from the heart of the country— until, in a sudden spurt, it became the dominant theme of fall releases of 1984.

Critics dismissed the farm-wife trend with a sniff, as so much shallow Hollywood posturing. But these roles were actually much more than that. The appeal of playing inelegant farm wives to actresses at the height of their fame transcends sentiment. The American farm wife harkens back to a day when being a mother was an economic necessity, not a form of schizophrenia—a mainstay in a now-forgotten world where family and work were one, and motherhood and wifehood could take on heroic proportions.

Unlike *Frances*, *The Postman Always Rings Twice*, or any of her other films, this movie was going to be about something real, about people she knew, the kind of people she grew up with, the kind of people she still saw at Christmas. Lange, an intelligent woman, had never finished college, and appeared in purely popular entertainment all of her professional life. She had made it. Now she would justify having made it. It was not turning her back on Hollywood—she was, after all, still making a movie—but it might have been, in fact, a way of orienting herself in the onslaught of all this superstardom, a way of not losing her soul.

On the other hand, producing your own independent film is a form of self-induced insanity. It means attending to every detail, from the first scripts and location scouting to hiring— and firing—your talent and crew, to final editing, distribution, and publicity—and Jessica would come up against all of this in the year following her Oscar. It means dealing with studios, distributors, theater owners, actors, writers, cameramen, gaffers, millions and millions of dollars of other people's money, and trying to keep some semblance of normalcy in your own life as well.

A single word balances the host of negatives: control. Lange had learned from *Frances.* No one was going to cross her interpretation or edit her performance to shreds again. Like Goldie Hawn, Jane Fonda, and Barbra Streisand, she joined the ranks of actress/producers. "I'm not sure I fulfilled the traditional role of the producer, you know, sitting in a big office making decisions about the Teamsters," Lange told the *Washington Post.* "But I was involved in the creative process from the inception to the release, and the film is close to what I wanted. A lot of care and love was put into it. I think it was done for the right reasons and it was done honestly."

If Lange wanted to do more than just act, she certainly got her chance in the making of *Country.* She lost her first studio, Ladd. Then her director, Hal Ashby, backed out. That meant her project was in turnaround, the name for a project once accepted and then rejected by a studio (rather like being divorced—it means somebody liked you once). Fortunately, she quickly got a second studio, Disney, looking for new material for their new label, Touchstone. Wittliff, they decided, could make his directorial debut with the film.

That summer, Lange talked to countless Iowa farm wives. She and Wittliff developed a story line about a typical Iowa farm family—two growing kids, a baby, father, grandpa, mom —whose farm begins to be swallowed up under the load of debt accumulated under the FHA. One neighbor commits suicide when his loans are called in. When it becomes clear that their equipment, if not all their land, will be auctioned to cover $96,000 in loans, Gil Ivy, the father, played by Shepard, takes to drinking and abusing his son. Jewell Ivy, played by Lange, tries to rally her neighbors to their cause and succeeds in gathering them to shout "No Sale!" at an auction of the Ivys' farm equipment. Lange's acting coach, Sandra Seacat, took the part of another beleagured farm wife whose son is retarded and whose husband commits suicide. The picture ends inconclusively, with the Ivys still struggling and a comment that the Justice Department had since ordered that farmers get due process of the law before their loans are called in.

Settling into the Waterloo Holiday Inn just in time for the autumn harvest of 1983, things got off to a rocky start when Lange fired Wittliff ten days into shooting. She thought he was softening the material, making the story too easy. "Jessica just didn't like what she saw in the dailies," Sam Shepard said, "and that was flat *it*, you know?" Richard Pearce (*Heartland*) was dispatched to replace Wittliff within a few short days and Shepard, one assumes, took on any last-minute rewriting chores as Wittliff departed the set.

But there was more trouble in store. Shooting in a small Iowa town, Lange, Shepard, and crew found that the winter of 1983 was the coldest in Iowa history. The physical harshness of the early winter would become an important character in the film and in their lives for the next three months. Shooting on location was important to Lange—she vowed at the film's outset that no scene would take place on a sound stage. It was important that the look be authentic—locals would chuckle at the clothing purchased new for Miss Lange and then scrubbed and washed to appear aged enough for the film. A local boy, Levi Knebel, starred as the sensitive teenage son. Richard Pearce, a former cameraman whose portrayal of nineteenth-century homestead life in *Heartland* had won him national attention as a director, turned the same, often stationary camera he had used in the earlier film to his contemporary subjects. Iowa became a still stretch of field and farm through his eyes —a calm at the center of an economic hurricane.

Temperatures plummeted. The emotional auction scene, using 100 local neighbors, took place in 25-below-zero weather. Shooting had to break every five minutes so that everyone could race to the barn and try to warm up around butane heaters. The snow here was not the kind a Hollywood film crew was usually offered. This was the first real stuff, freezing cast and crew and threatening expensive camera equipment. "The fact that all of this was happening in a town called Waterloo was not lost on anyone," commented then Disney president Richard Berger wryly. One of those chilly afternoons, Sam Shepard received divorce papers from his wife, O-lan, from a messenger who slipped past the tight security by posing as an extra. It would be many long and difficult months before their separation would be final in July 1984.

Filming a picture with the country's most romantic couple when the girlfriend is the producer had built-in hazards of its own, director Pearce discovered. He made it a condition of the film that he deal separately with Lange and Shepard in rehearsing scenes and other matters. The lovers had very different approaches to the film. Lange, Pearce described in Don Shewey's *Sam Shepard* (Dell Publishing Co., 1985), was "a very disciplined actress, very smart, very prepared, and she's the producer of the film and can't goof off. Then her co-star, and the man she lives with, and the man she fights with and screws and whatever else, is arriving late, trying to devise strategies to relax everybody, to loosen the process up." Shepard was also on call for the intensive rewriting on *Paris, Texas*, which German director Wim Wenders was doing on Shepard's original script, shooting simultaneously in Texas. Nonetheless, "It worked," Pearce said, "because they're alive when they're together and they're alive on the screen when they're together."

In December, *Country* itself abandoned the country, as the film was forced to depart Iowa because of the cold and finish shooting on a reconstructed farmhouse at Disney's studios in Los Angeles. The opening tornado scene, the last scene to be shot, took place on a half-acre cornfield on a Disney sound stage, under the blast of six wind machines.

Finally, $2 million over budget and thirty-five days late, *Country* was delivered to its studio overseers at Walt Disney's new Touchstone label. This was to be Disney's second release under their new adult label, and it made a sharp contrast to their first film, *Splash*, a lighthearted and very profitable fantasy about a mermaid in New York (at a much earlier stage in her career, just after *King Kong*, Jessica Lange was considered for the lead in just such a mermaid film!).

Pondering the dark nature of this film, the Disney brass

planned a slow rollout across the country, hoping the movie would find a serious filmgoing audience through word-of-mouth. To that end, *Country* was entered in the New York Film Festival and chosen to be its opening night film, a prestigious, black-tie event that took place in Manhattan's Lincoln Center for members of the Lincoln Center Film Society.

Lange and Shepard, meanwhile, headed for a Beacon Hill brownstone and a more civilized environment in Boston, where Shepard was playwright-in-residence for a month at the American Repertory Theater in Cambridge. Conveniently enough (or perhaps not so conveniently), Baryshnikov was also in residence in Boston with the American Ballet Theater, and Shura, by this time an articulate little three-year-old, dropped by almost every afternoon with her nanny to watch Daddy and his dancers rehearse. Lange also occasionally brought the child to ABT performances. "I want her to understand what her father does," Lange said. Shepard, for his part, angrily fended off photographers who hovered around their exclusive Beacon Hill home in hopes of snapping a photo of the celebrity couple. Lange merely pleaded quietly to be left alone.

Neither Shepard nor Lange could complain, for they were selling themselves to sell *Country*. Or rather, Lange persuaded her reclusive co-star to help publicize the film both with her and on his own. Having refused all publicity chores for *The Right Stuff*, including turning down a *Newsweek* cover story, Shepard agreed to be interviewed for a cover story for *American Film* at Lange's request. The two were also photographed by Bruce Weber, the famed fashion photographer, who arrived at their New Mexico ranch and immortalized the famous lovers in fine-grained, black-and-white photographs that appeared in the October *Vanity Fair*. All Lange's publicity savvy was brought to bear on *Country*—savvy born, no doubt, of having been the pawn in one of the great publicity drives of all time, the selling of Dino De Laurentiis's 1976 *King Kong*. After hiring New York publicist Marion Billings to handle *Country*'s publicity, Lange brought a New York photographer friend down to her ranch for another lavish spread that would appear in the October issue of *Vogue*.

In *Vogue*, Lange revealed her beauty regimen: nothing. No makeup, no formal exercises except riding, long walks in the country, and swimming a mile a day, a vegetarian diet adhered to from her hippie days. Her smoking habit had gone by the boards with impending motherhood. "As far as looks, on the most superficial level, no, I don't think about them at all," she told *Vogue*'s Karen Anderegg. "I'll tell you one thing, as an actress you're sitting in the makeup chair and working all day in front of the cameras and watching the dailies after. I mean, I get sick of myself, I really do."

Sam didn't. He even managed to attend the opening night festivities, which was more than he'd done for the premiere of *The Right Stuff* or his own Academy Award nomination that April. His second volume of plays appeared that December dedicated "To Jessica." Titled *Fool for Love* after his play, the book began with an epigraph from Archbishop Anthony Bloom: "The proper response to love is to accept it. There is nothing to *do*."

It may have made sound film business sense for *Country* to open the New York Film Festival on September 28, 1984, but aesthetically, it couldn't have been more off-cue. After watching the grueling, humorless film of an issue that defied entertainment, the most demanding film fans in the world shuffled past the Lincoln Center fountain to the Vivian Beaumont Theater for a massive party. Every variant of black dress known to womankind played a sharp contrast to Jessica Lange's shapeless plaids just seen onscreen. So, too, did tables heaped with chic caterer Dean and DeLuca's imported cheeses, fruits, and desserts, mocking the hamburgers on white bread that Jewell Ivy feeds her family, a combination which, one suspects, most of the audience had never even thought of, let alone eaten.

Somehow, the whole enterprise rang false. Jessica Lange, in a beaded black dress, and Sam Shepard, in the requisite tuxedo, made their way to the party through a long corridor, surrounded by paparazzi, Shepard with his arm around Lange and a look on his face exactly like a basketball star trying to protect his girl from local thugs as they make their way to the high-school prom. They were story-book sweethearts—photographers could charge high prices for any pictures of the two of them together—and that was all that mattered. People were simply disbelieving of the emotions of the film. To most of them, the world depicted in *Country* was not a real world.

Concurrent with the opening was a series of press conferences and a daylong session with nearly one hundred out-of-town journalists. Lange was "quite impressive" in handling the inevitable questions about the troubles on the *Country* set, according to the Film Festival's director of publicity, Joanna Ney. "She was very much in command," Ney said. "She was very cooperative and nice, very straightforward and honest. But she wasn't all that chatty—she's obviously a very private person."

The film's premiere in Iowa was a far more moving experience, and a major social event for Des Moines. "This film was so true to life and so accurate that words cannot do justice to its emotional impact," wrote *The Farm Journal*'s Greg Wood of a screening with three hundred Iowa farm families in Des Moines. "Men and women alike cried, including this reviewer, who has never cried at a movie in his life." Among the nation's million or so farmers, the film became required viewing. Farmers, "obviously reliving their own struggles for survival," wrote Wood, cheered and applauded throughout the film.

As with *Kong,* however, all the publicity in the world couldn't reach the people who basically didn't want to see the film. Hers fared the worst of the so-called "Dust Bowl Trilogy," though Lange was nominated for the second time for best actress, losing to Sally Field, whose on-camera gushing was obviously not Jessica's style. "*Country,*" Lange insisted to the press, "is very unlike those others. It's unfortunate we're being lumped together as farm films."

Once again, Lange was cited as the reason to see the movie. "She is a force of nature," wrote Canby. "Even in pink curlers," wrote Pauline Kael, "Lange looks ready to break the bank at Monte Carlo." The other reason, of course, was to see the two lovers on screen together. The screen, however, did not steam up. The two had "drained all the sex appeal out of themselves to the point that drabness becomes an affectation," wrote *Vogue.* "This earnest movie about the financial plight of Midwestern farmers just sits there, too conscious of being honorable to be fun."

But, according to Lange, working with Shepard, not surprisingly, was a good experience that benefited the film. "I think there was something that was established between these two characters on-screen, just in the subtleties and the nuances, because we know each other and because we are together," she told the "Today" show's Gene Shalit in October 1985. "You could see that these people had some history and knew each other and lived together."

In the end, the most satisfying part of making *Country* for Lange was the response of the farmers themselves. "I got letters and calls and just extraordinary response from them about somebody taking the time and telling their story and how deeply they were affected by it," she told Shalit.

How seriously Lange took this cause was evident when she came armed with a ten-page position paper to read to the House Agricultural Subcommittee that May. In a moving account where Lange broke down in tears, she told of meeting farm wives as she researched her film. Along with Jane Fonda and Sissy Spacek, her Hollywood reputation got the cause on the evening news on all three networks. While Fonda, in the background, wiped away tears, Lange, in a cornflower-blue dress and no makeup, spoke fervently, in a speech she wrote herself on the plane from Albuquerque to Washington, D.C., of the need for the government to rework the economics of farming. "I've seen over and over the toll that living with the terrible fear of losing everything takes on these proud people," she said. During the testimony, Lange recalled, "I got very emotional . . . and then, once my part was completed, I felt an immediate rush of exhilaration, like I had done something. It was a great sensation."

Picking and choosing among the welter of projects available to her, Lange said yes only to those projects that challenged her as an actress. In between the stay in Boston and *Country*'s opening in September of 1984, for example, Lange took on the part of Maggie the Cat in a remake of the Tennessee Williams Play *Cat on a Hot Tin Roof* for the pay-movie channel Showtime's series, "Broadway on Showtime," a co-production with PBS's "American Playhouse." Unlike the well-known film version starring Paul Newman and Elizabeth Taylor, this *Cat* got to keep all its claws; it was to contain all of Williams's original language, including its references to homosexuality, and the ending which the playwright originally intended (director Elia Kazan had ordered a softened, more optimistic

ending for the earlier version). Lange's acceptance of the part
—at a fraction of the price she could have commanded—surprised and delighted Showtime officials and brought with it a
bevy of equally low-priced stars happy to reduce their normal
wages to work on a project with Jessica Lange. "Let's be
honest about it," said Phylis Geller, the producer. "Jessica
opened the floodgates for us. Before she signed, there was great
concern over getting actors with box-office name value, but
once she said yes, that was enough."

Kim Stanley joined her as Big Mama, with Treat Williams
as the homosexual husband and Rip Torn as Big Daddy in the
story of a powerful, dying man and the conflict of his sons and
their wives on a Southern plantation. Jim Hofsiss (who directed the stage version of *The Elephant Man*) directed. The
production was taped in Los Angeles, a town which never
brought out the best in Lange to begin with. She and Shepard
holed up in the penthouse of the Chateau Marmont (the same
hotel where John Belushi died) for part of the stay. The three
weeks of rehearsal and six days of shooting at Hollywood's
KZEX studios culminated in two evenings where work continued until one-thirty in the morning. Reports surfaced, once
again, that Jessica was being "difficult," but, by this point in
her career, Lange did not have to defend her approach to
acting, which included lying down between takes with her
head in her hands. The critics praised her performance when
the program played on Showtime in August 1984, though a
few called it overdrawn. "If Lange initially seems in danger of
sinking in Southern quicksand," wrote *Time* magazine's Richard Zoglin, "she soon gains her footing and brings one of
Williams's most memorable roles to stunning life." Lange
thought it her best acting yet—"perhaps better than *Frances*,"
she told one reporter.

Lange delighted another cable company, HBO, when she agreed to play the leading role of Patsy Cline in a film released by Tristar on the legendary country singer's life, written by Robert Gretchell, whose script for *Alice Doesn't Live Here Anymore* had been nominated for an Oscar. "We've always been great fans of hers," said HBO Pictures President Steve Scheffer, whose company shares ownership of Tristar with Coca-Cola and CBS, "and we thought this was a role she might respond to." Scheffer had run into Lange's agent, Lou Pitt, at a screening for HBO's miniseries *The Far Pavilions* back when the Lange project was still being called *The Patsy Cline Story*, and mentioned the script. Pitt thought the idea was a long shot, but then he didn't know of Lange's lifelong secret ambition to play a country singer. What he did know was that his lovely client was notoriously tone-deaf. No problem, said the HBO producers. After all, Audrey Hepburn had made it through the Academy Award-winning *My Fair Lady* without singing a note. Jessica accepted the part a few days later.

As it turned out, a solution to the voice problem presented itself rather adroitly. Patsy's voice had been recorded on a separate track on her original recordings back in the early sixties. Jessica could lip-synch the words and the new instrumental tracks would be dubbed in with up-to-date acoustical standards.

The story revolved around the tempestuous singer's rise to fame and love affair and eventual marriage to her second husband, Charlie Dick, before her death at age thirty. Finding the right leading man turned out to be a bit of a problem. Jessica's original choice for leading man, over which she presumably had some say, was, naturally, Sam Shepard, but Shepard, perhaps weary from the months spent on *Country,* and ready to direct his own film version of *Fool for Love,* turned that idea down. "She wanted me to do this part," he said in *American Film*, "another one of these guys who's so screwed up he beats her up; she's the martyred woman and all. I just figured I didn't want to do that." Then Kurt Russell was cast for the role, but backed out. Finally, Ed Harris—a Sam Shepard favorite, who had won an Obie for his male lead in the New York production of *Fool for Love*—took the role. Karol Reisz, the Czech director who wrote the classic film text *The Technique of Editing* and who had directed several well-received films, including *Morgan, Who'll Stop The Rain?* and *The French Lieutenant's Woman*, was set to direct. The producer was Bernard Schwartz, who had been working on the project for months and had overseen Beverly D'Angelo's scene-stealing portrait of Patsy Cline as Loretta Lynn's best friend in his production of the Oscar-winning *Coal Miner's Daughter*.

Lange, the former student of mime, worked with Cline's own singing coach, Owen Bradford, to get the singer's inflections and gestures right and grilled Cline's acquaintances and old friends for clues about how Patsy Cline moved onstage and off. Lange herself mastered seventeen of Cline's memorable tunes—among them "I Fall to Pieces," "Sweet Dreams," "Crazy," and "Walkin' After Midnight." During filming, she belted them out in her own voice, so that the muscles of her face and neck looked realistic when Cline's voice emerged from them. Lange was so embarrassed about the quality of her own voice, however, that she always made sure the recording of Cline blared out enough to drown her out! The final results impressed even Patsy Cline's mother, watching on location in West Virginia: "She belts out the songs just like Patsy did." Certainly, no viewer of the film would suspect that here was a woman who was so timid about her singing voice that the only person she'd sing aloud to was her daughter Shura.

Lange put on some twenty-five pounds and dyed her hair dark brown for the part. "She really got into the role," Scheffer said. The crew went on location for three weeks to the tiny burg of Martinsburg, West Virginia, very near Cline's own hometown, where 600 of the town's 13,000 inhabitants got roles as extras. Though, one evening shooting lasted until 4 A.M. and ended with Harris pelting a shot glass through a mirror in a bar, for the most part, this shoot was an easy task for Lange. After a year and a half of shouldering responsibility for *Country*, it was a relief simply to act. The HBO brass were enthusiastic. "This is going to be the *Places in the Heart* of 1985," said Scheffer. "If she doesn't win an Oscar for this, I'll be very, very surprised."

Unfortunately, in an apparently unbreakable trend, Lange's performance outpaced the film that contained it, at least according to reviewers when the film was released in early October of 1985. Praise for Lange ran high, for the film, less so, and the results at the box office were not impressive. "*Sweet Dreams* is worth seeing for the acting," wrote Jan Hoffmann in the *Village Voice*, "but if you want to hear about the life and loves of Patsy Cline, an album is about the same price as a ticket." The Gretchell script concentrated on the love story to such an extent that Cline's career almost comes as an afterthought. Nonetheless, Lange gives what is possibly the most winning, all-embracing performance of her career. Patsy Cline is surely one of the most three-dimensional, recognizable women on a movie screen in a long time, and an intriguing contrast to Meryl Streep's offering for that same autumn, the ice queen neurotic of *Plenty*. Ann Wedgeworth, as Cline's mother, "displays a lovely rapport with Miss Lange," wrote *The New York Times*'s Janet Maslin. Jessica Lange is "sultry, nervy, delicate and altogether amazing," gushed Peter Travers in *People*.

In conjunction with the opening of *Sweet Dreams*, a six-months-pregnant Jessica showed up at the Kennedy Center in Washington, D.C., to receive an award from the Congressional Arts Caucus, whose executive committee boasts two congressmen from Minnesota. The award was offered "in recognition for outstanding portrayals of American women in film and dedication to excellence in the finest tradition of the American theater." Lange wore a black velvet smock top and black stovepipe pants, her hair light and curled, her face beaming. "The operable thing to consider in the presence of Jessica Lange," reported one *Time* executive who attended the black-tie affair, "is to remain standing up."

Naturally, both the entertainment and serious literary worlds alike have awaited some collaboration between Shepard and Lange—one not fulfilled in the filmed version of Shepard's play *Fool for Love*, which opened in December 1985 and starred Kim Basinger in the female lead and Shepard in the male lead. But that's probably because of another collaboration —the second child that Lange has always told reporters she planned to have. The child, Hannah Jane, who bears Shepard's surname and is half-sibling to his fifteen-year-old son Jesse and Lange's daughter Shura, was born in mid-January of 1986.

Just one year before, Lange had vowed to the *Washington Post*'s David Richards, "These are the last words out of my mouth—forever. I really feel I've exhausted the subject of my life. I'm beginning to bore myself." But Lange is a professional, and consented to yet another round of interviews to publicize *Sweet Dreams*. Besides the highly publicized testimony in front of the Congressional subcommittee that spring, by October of 1985, Lange had another five-day stint on the "Today" show with Gene Shalit, along with a surprisingly confessional interview in *The New York Times*. Meanwhile, Sam Shepard finally appeared on the cover of *Newsweek* to publicize his film *Fool for Love.*

Anyone waiting for these two to break up so as to reactivate the fantasy lives of the average American male and female had their hopes dashed by the *Newsweek* article. Lange told *Newsweek*'s Jack Kroll: "Sam was like something I was looking for all my life and never came upon in its entirety. I've always been so restless, so on the run, never really feeling connected with anything. But with him—one day I just woke up and realized it had happened, after dreaming about it all these years." "I would have been down the river if I hadn't met Jessica," declared Shepard. "This is the first time in twenty years that I've felt I had a home," echoed Lange, "that there's this place and this family where I belong." Both were settling down, they declared, after years of self-inflicted romantic turmoil.

Romance used to be defined by conflict, Lange told Dena Kleiman of *The New York Times.* "It was a trap for me. As long as it was passionate. Either positive or negative. Then I knew it was love. It had to be extreme. That was its validity. As soon as anything became too settled, too regular, too placid, I'd have to get in there with the Mixmaster to make sure things were still cooking." Now, however, Lange calls Sam, Shura, Hannah Jane, and herself "a real family," and says she plans to take care of Shepard for the rest of her life. Marriage is "an absolute possibility," if not officially in the wings.

Work has changed as well for Lange since the days when she would exhaust herself making *Frances* and *Tootsie* back to back in a single year. At this level of superstardom, there's only one reason to work: because she wants to. "I don't want to work for the money," Lange told *The New York Times.* "I don't want to work for the work. I don't need to validate my existence." A project, at this point, has to justify time away from her two children and dragging Shura out of school. Not surprisingly, very few projects have attracted her imagination. Most scripts have "the dispensable female lead," Lange said. "They could be played by anybody."

Looking for the indispensable female lead, Lange optioned the novel *Machine Dreams*, from the highly respected young fiction writer Jayne Anne Phillips, in the spring of 1984. It is logically a vehicle for herself and Sam Shepard, though they have announced no plans to that end. The purchase confirms her unerring taste, for it is another paradigmatic tale, of war and two generations—a good war for the father in World War II, and a bad war, in Vietnam, for his son. Phillips declined to write the screenplay, so Lange decided to write the script herself—a first for her—over the summer in New Mexico. The first draft was completed by the October opening duties of *Sweet Dreams*.

Can directing be far behind? "She should be a director," enthused Shepard in *American Film*. "She's got a great eye." "Not for awhile," answers Lange in her publicity material for *Country*. "There's a lot that I would like to learn, that I would have to learn, before I would think of attempting directing. It amazes me how many people just jump into directing a film. Directing is an art and not something just anyone can do." But production is still the logical route for Lange's talents, perhaps under the aegis of her own production company.

Another project Lange has gendered enthusiasm for is the upcoming film version of Beth Henley's *Crimes of the Heart*, the Pulitzer Prize-winning play about three sisters, which is slated to co-star Diane Keaton and Sissy Spacek and be directed by the Australian director Bruce Beresford (*Tender Mercies*), and begin shooting in April. Lange plays the sister accused of murdering her husband. The chance to do ensemble acting with her peers appealed to her. "I'm excited about doing a piece with other women for a change," Lange told Gene Siskel. "I'm tired of biographies and I'm tired of playing the strong woman supporting the weaker man."

In the meantime, time was definitely taken off for her second child, Hannah Jane, born in Santa Fe, a healthy seven pounds, four ounces, last winter. Preceding their daughter's birth, Shepard and Lange lived in Manhattan for several weeks in the late fall of 1985 as Shepard prepared a new play, *A Lie of the Mind,* with an all-star cast. Shura attended "pre-kindergarten" school, while Lange tolerated paparazzi who flashed bulbs in her face when she ran errands on Fifty-seventh Street. Shura, by now, enjoyed a "powerful relationship" with her dad, Mikhail Baryshnikov, Lange told the "Today" show's Gene Shalit, while Shepard had become "a great pal." "She's the envy of a lot of girls," quipped Shalit.

Sweet Dreams, Machine Dreams—the dreams are a reality now. "I've realized that with the last year and a half or two years that I had no more true unhappiness in my life," Lange said in a recent interview in *Vogue,* "and I've always lived with unhappiness. Suddenly, I can honestly say, really, for the first time in my life, that I'm very happy."

There's a reason good stories stop at "happily ever after." Once Jessica Lange makes it, her story somehow loses its spunk. The struggle is over. She's perfect. She does politically correct movies. She lives on the land. She has her children, her horses, her homes in New Mexico and Minnesota, the adoration of a brilliant lover, the esteem of her peers and public.

No, the fun began a long time ago—a long, bumpy time ago —with Jessica before she was a blonde starlet, or a blonde star, or a superstar—before, in fact, she was blonde at all. Before her name had gained a syllable, when everyone who knew her called her, simply, "Jessie." The years when she was merely one of thousands of young Americans relishing an experience as have few generations before or since: dropping out.

6

WANDERING YEARS

The University of Minnesota's fifty-thousand student Minneapolis campus is serviced by a small commercial area fondly dubbed "Dinkytown" after one George Dinky, who must have had something to do with the place at one time or another. The U of M, as it is known, occupies a part of Minneapolis that borders the white bluffs of the Mississippi River. Dinkytown is no Cambridge, or Berkeley or even Madison, the neighboring school that had already done its share to put student protests on the map by 1967—it is instead a somber place, influenced by the hard-working, rather unimaginative nature of the Scandinavian settlers who founded it. Most of the students hang out with their former high-school crowd; many live at home. Boring lecture classes can be whiled away by picking out the one hundred shades of natural blonde that grace the backs of bent heads. The greatest challenge is surviving the winter trimester that spans the subzero eternity between Minnesota's January and Minnesota's March. And, unquestionably, April is the cruelest month: There's always another snowstorm.

One of those winter quarters is enough to convince most people with any stretch of imagination that there has got to be a better way to spend the winter. Jessica Lange, a freshman with sleek, shoulder-length brown hair in the fall of 1967, was no exception.

"She was arty as hell," a professor remembers. "She looked like the perfect U of M coed who comes from a small town and wants to be groovy and did whatever the hell you had to do to be that." She was supposed to be painting. She was there, after all, as her tiny high school's honor student on an art scholarship. She had always wanted to be a painter, even as a child. "I was very good and I was immersed in it," Lange recalled. "I looked ahead to a very safe life in an academic setting where my work would keep me from getting bored."

Of course, a school of fifty thousand students can make the study of drawing a little tough. The university art department, in order to keep its incipient art population to a manageable level, insisted that one beginning drawing class had to be taken by everyone before they could take anything else. The classes filled up within fifteen minutes of the opening of registration, and for the next few weeks art professors who taught the drawing classes were inundated with students begging to be let in.

Jessie, initially, didn't get in. "I'll never forget it," laughs a former professor of hers, Thomas Egerman. "I had a sign up on the door—class is full. This trim young woman came up to me, looked me straight in the eye, and said: 'I will do *anything* to get into your art class.' " Egerman, taken aback by her directness, "almost fainted!" She got in.

That was Jessie Lange. She wore blue jeans and a 1940s-style fur coat. "She was not the best-looking girl in the class, by any means," her professor remembers. "I wasn't overwhelmed or anything. When *King Kong* came out, it never occurred to me that she was the same person."

The university art department was an exciting place in the

late sixties. A score of bright, young artists had been invited to teach there. Lange dutifully sketched three times a week for two hours. By reports, she was a serious, good, but not exceptional, student. When the second trimester rolled around, the winter quarter's art classes were just as closed as before. Lange complained in frustration to her first-term professor that she couldn't get into a class taught by one Mario Volper. "That teacher," chuckled her first professor, "dressed like a French lawyer and he liked beautiful women. I told her that she should apply anyway, and she got into that class, too!"

But it was not those drawing classes that had the most important lesson in store for Lange. One of the young teachers had brought in a guest professor for a photography class. His name was Paco Grande. The darkly handsome twenty-four-year-old Spaniard came from a wealthy Castillian family. His was an international identity, belonging to a fledgling avant-garde that was spanning the Atlantic. To Jessie Lange, sitting in on his class, he was remarkably exotic. There had been nothing like him in her tiny northern Minnesota hometown of Cloquet. He wasn't Swedish or Norwegian or even Finnish.

"Northern Minnesota was homogenous," Lange told *The New York Times* years later, "and I was swept off my feet by this handsome Spaniard I met during my first year of college." Grande talked art. He talked music. He talked film. By this time, Jessica was into astrology—herself, born on April 20, an obvious Taurus—but Paco introduced her to the *I Ching*, giving her a copy that she carried with her for years afterward. He was a Scorpio. "I have a long history of Scorpios," Lange explained to one interviewer. "I guess I'm attracted to Europeans basically. I guess that's odd. . . ." A more important catalyst kicked into effect here, one that Lange, who never so much as finished a single year of college, returned to in love after love. "I seem to be attracted to people who have some information," Lange observed of herself, "something to teach me." She was the autodidact, the self-teacher, a classic case of the middle-class girl determined to better herself, rather like an updated version of a Trollope heroine. She had great intelligence—she's certainly smarter than any film character she has ever played—and deep curiosity, with high standards for herself that she knew she could reach only with the help of the right men. So lovers were men who could satisfy her mind as well as her body, teachers as well as lovers. And when they had no more to teach—or when she had no more to learn—she moved on.

Lesson number one began with Paco, and it lasted, off and on, for five years. Though it would end bitterly in 1982, in a highly publicized divorce instigated only after Lange had Baryshnikov's child, for many years the match was "passionate, intense, and loving," Lange would say later.

Paco, as Lange described him, was "a very interesting person, one of the most intelligent people I know." Grande, known and recognized by others in the New York and European underground film community, "was always into new things before they became hip or mainstream," Lange said. "Country music, reggae, art, everything." She would say in 1983, in an interview after *Frances*, "I miss him every day." His blindness, the result of a degenerative eye disease, retinitis pigmentosa, was not in evidence in those years. If anything, he opened this Cloquet girl's eyes to things she had never dreamed of.

One of the first things he taught Jessie was that there were better places to be than Minnesota—in the winter or any other time. By March, in what would have been the second trimester of her freshman year, Jessica said good-bye to her parents, brother and two big sisters, and departed Minnesota. First, the two lovers dropped anchor in a city known for another kind of coldness, a coldness Lange would get to know as well as Minnesota's over the years: New York.

By May of 1968, they reached Paris. Jessie and Paco watched, like a latter-day John Reed and Louise Bryant, as the Marxist student leader Danny the Red and his radical student/worker followers tore the cobblestone streets apart and battled police. The eighteen-year-old promised herself, as do most first-time visitors to the city, to return to Paris, one day, to live. She and Paco then took off to visit friends, mostly avant-garde filmmakers, from all over Europe "who were committed to their work," Lange said. Indeed, it was a time of passionate commitments. "I don't think Jessica was ever really a radical," recalled one old friend who knew her then. And yet the moral stance infected her. "We were violent idealists," she recalled after her stardom was assured, on the "Today" show in 1983. "I was very much a part of it—thank God. I thank God it didn't pass me by."

But, in a Pierre Hotel suite in 1977, at the end of her grueling, six-week publicity tour for *King Kong*, an exhausted Lange gave the camera a look of piercing world-weariness, shrugged, and summed up her travels while chain-smoking Marlboro Lights. "It's very boring, in a way," she began, " . . . but what I did then was to go to Europe for six months, then university for another quarter, then to New York to study dance, moved to San Francisco, moved to Mexico, came back to New York City, went to Paris for two years and came back to New York City and then to Paris and then New York."

Actually, it was anything but boring. In their own version

of Jack Kerouac's *On the Road*, Lange and Grande zigzagged across the country, living on next to nothing, sleeping in the back of their own van. Days would pass when their only companionship would be each other. The two depended on each other for everything. When Lange and Grande arrived in Marin County to visit her sister Jane, Lange recalled, "She said it was as if two people had ceased to exist and there was a new entity." (Later, after *Kong*, after she'd met Baryshnikov and lived without Paco for four years, in her interviews about this time, Lange didn't mention Paco unless someone brought him up. She said she traveled with "friends or my boyfriend.")

In New Mexico for the first time, Jessie's painter's eye detected the same pristine beauty that had drawn Georgia O'Keeffe to this blistering American landscape. She vowed to return there, too.

Paco and Lange were married on July 29, 1970, in a simple ceremony in her parents' home in Lake Nebagomen, Wisconsin, shortly after what would have been her sophomore year. That was followed by six months in Spain, Malaysia, and Amsterdam. They often traveled with underground filmmaker friends of Paco's, "making these bizarre, esoteric little films" across Europe. Jessie tagged along, her *I Ching* in hand.

Home base, by now, was Soho—a since-vanished Soho, as it was before this part of lower Manhattan became a southern outpost for Fifth Avenue and Fifty-seventh Street. Artists settled in Soho in the sixties because the lofts, abandoned by industry, were cheap and had huge windows that let in light for painting. Lange and Paco lived in a loft with neighbors like Kate Millet, friends like Allan Shields, and other painters, performers, and hangers-on of a then-obscure but fertile downtown scene. Paco, devoted as always to his work, supported himself as a photographer. Ellie Klein, a dancer who had been with Merce Cunningham, was forming her own troupe and Jessie joined that.

In those years, Lange floundered around for a cause that equaled that of the obsessed, impassioned artists she'd been meeting through Paco—and that of Paco himself. There is nothing quite as debilitating for a creative person as being the lover of someone whose creative career is in better shape than one's own. Whatever it was—film, dance, radical politics— Jessie lacked some essential ingredient. It wasn't talent, exactly. "I realized I didn't have a commitment," she said. "And I began looking for one. I realized that whatever talent I had for painting and sculpture was lacking in the most vital of all ingredients, commitment. . . . I had been looking for safe surroundings in a university environment. The people who were really into the arts were not seeking safety. This fact was constantly driven home to me, more so when we returned to New York and lived in Soho."

Whatever it was, painting was definitely not it: "I didn't have this emotional commitment to paint that I saw all around me," Lange would tell David Richards of the *Washington Post* a decade later. "I don't think I was ever that good. Oh, I pretended to be. I did very abstract stuff, these awful minimal sculptures—Formica boxes in primary colors. I don't know where any of them are now. The last thing somebody told me was that they had found one of my Formica boxes, which I considered my greatest work of art, and had used it a while as a coffee table, and then thrown it out when it got dirty. That's an appropriate demise for my art career."

Lange began to think of herself as a dancer instead. She had studied a little dance as a child, though, being in her early twenties, she was far too old to undertake a serious career, even as a modern dancer. Nonetheless, her dance troupe was one of dozens of little experimental dance groups that sprouted throughout lower Manhattan in the late sixties and early seventies,and the troupe began to experiment with mime, the stylized mimicry of motion by the human body. This was long before Marcel Marceau had become a household name, before mime was used to sell IBM personal computers. Just about the only place to see mime was in movies from abroad—as in Antonioni's *Blow-Up*, in which a mime troupe ended the picture hitting an imaginary tennis ball across a court—or in the most famous film of all with mime: *Les Enfants du Paradis*, or *The Children of Paradise*. Marcel Carne's film, an elaborate tale of a nineteenth-century actress and the men who loved her, had been made under great hardship during the occupation of France by the Nazis, and became one of the classics of cinema upon its release in 1945. Jean-Louis Barrault starred as the great French mime, Debureau, in love with the fickle Arletty. When Lange saw it, she fell in love with mime.

"It remains my favorite of all films," Lange said. "It was the most beautiful film I had ever seen." An avid filmgoer, married to a filmmaker, Lange had seen many movies, but nothing that affected her like this. She walked out onto the New York streets after the movie ended, in a trance. Horns honked, men whistled, but Jess didn't hear them. "I was torn apart, I was in a spell," she effused. "I felt that for this first time in my life I had a grasp of where I could seek commitment."

Mime was it. This language of motion, the physical, totally silent expression of imagination, struck something in Jessie that music, painting, photography couldn't. Mime is the art of imitation, something that Jess had been learning from and would continue to learn from for years. The new kid in school mimics those around her so she doesn't stick out, and Jess had always been the new kid, in a family that moved every year. It was dance with meaning, acting without words. Mime was it.

Eager to take her rightful place in the ranks of artists with a commitment, Lange became a convert seeking knowledge. She wanted to know everything about mime, about its traditions and its background, about how Barrault had learned mime. Who were the great teachers?

"And I finally uncovered the great secret. The man was Etienne Decroux. He taught Barrault and he was the best." After years of trailing after Paco, Jessie knew what she wanted to do. She would study mime, and she would study it with Decroux. There was only one problem. Decroux lived in Paris. If she wanted to meet this great artist, she would have to leave New York and go back, alone, to Paris.

All right, so be it. Lange booked a cheap flight, said goodbye to Paco and their friends, and boarded a plane for France with one suitcase and the money she had left to her name after paying for the flight. It was an abrupt decision, and typical of the always-determined Jessie—but not as hard to make as it might seem. The year was 1971. Nixon was in office. The war, immoral, apparently unstoppable, ground on in Vietnam. The fervor of the late sixties seemed to be on the wane in New York and everywhere else. Lange, who had departed in disgust from her hometown, then her home state, now had few compunctions about departing in disgust from her home country. The time to be an expatriate had arrived. "I had three hundred dollars in my pocketbook," Lange said. "I spoke no French. But I had a commitment."

7

PARIS AND MIME

In March even Paris lacks romance. Of course, the weather seemed fairly balmy to a native of Cloquet. Lange arrived, alone, and immediately took the hour-long ride on the metro to the suburb of Boulogne Billencourt, where Decroux lived in a little house. She had gotten the address from a friend in New York. She gingerly made her way downstairs to the basement where Decroux taught. It wasn't large, she noticed, just a bare studio. The first meeting was "humiliating for me," Lange remembered. "I spoke no French and he was insulted that I would dare approach him and speak English." Instead of welcoming this young pilgrim, one of the inventors of mime —which is what the former ballet dancer, now in his seventies, was—exploded. "He was vehement. There was no room for the likes of me." Jessie, crushed, turned to go back up the stairs.

But suddenly, inexplicably, the great master changed his mind and invited her to stay. Mademoiselle would have to learn French, he insisted, and Jessica eagerly agreed (this was the same French that would later serve her in getting to know a certain Russian dancer whose recent defection had left him ill-equipped to converse in English). Mime classes met in the basement early in the morning, six days a week, for which Decroux charged 100 francs a month. "To this day I don't know what made him change his mind," Lange said. But he did. She stayed for two years.

With the help of Paco's friends whom she had met in earlier travels, Jessie found a cold-water flat in the Fourth Arrondissement, a walk-up above a sausage factory, with no shower or bath. She borrowed books on French grammar. She converted her $300 into French francs that, with frugal habits, would last her half a year. And the next day, she took the metro back to Boulogne Billencourt, went back to the basement, took off her shoes, and began to study mime.

The young Americans, French, Swiss, Canadians, and other international explorers who sat at the feet of Etienne Decroux were definitely your "starving artist crowd," one veteran of those days recalls. "People came from all over the world to study with him," she remembers. "All these people who were floating around. It became a whole crowd of very close friends. It was a very strong bond, we had a great time." Probably everyone involved in those classes looks back at the years in Paris with a certain sweet heartache. Here the international language of acting was taught by the man who taught Marcel Marceau. Mime was always studied barefoot—motions of the ball and toe were intrinsic to the mime's "fake walk." Eager students sat cross-legged on the floor. Watching. Observing. Practicing. One of them has recalled, "We were all at his mercy and we all adored him." An uncompromising artist, Decroux also felt that Barrault had abandoned being a fine mime in order to become merely an actor. "Bah," said Decroux. "There are thousands of actors and very few mimes."

Mime is so foreign to American notions of acting that Lange's two years of study are generally dismissed as a kind of whim. In the magazine articles and publicity material generated for *King Kong,* it is scarcely mentioned at all. But Lange's commitment to mime was wholehearted; she was as dedicated to it as to anything else in her life. It was the beginning of her own intense study of acting; it was different from the Method approach, and its influence on her technique is evident to anyone who knows mime. The study is rigorous, the technique, strict. It is an attitude as well as an art. Its mark is visible in all her work.

For example, Lange is a very physical actress. In Lange's film work, a gesture nearly always precedes a sentence—whether it's her characteristic sidelong glance of the eyes, looking away from her subject just before, during, or after addressing him or her, or a splay of long fingers, a twist of her mouth —always some motion reinforces, contains, or connects the dialogue. Her use of larger physical motions can be extraordinarily vivid. In *Frances,* to pick one brief moment, she is waiting outside a mansion in a large car as a little man from the studio orders her to attend a party inside. He pulls open the car door and Lange's elbow sinks down where she had been leaning on the car door—a small moment, but a physical message of Frances's reluctance to go inside.

Her slouch and pout in *The Postman Always Rings Twice* would later strike Nicholson and Rafelson as clear evidence of her mime influence. At one point in *Postman,* Lange walks downstairs to get some milk after having made love to Nicholson for the first time earlier that day. She finds him sitting in the kitchen and stares at him lustfully while she goes to the icebox. Her hand misses the icebox door handle at first, then she comes to and opens the door, all the while still staring at Nicholson. That kind of physical detail—which Rafelson himself thought she had done by mistake until he saw the rushes —comes from mime.

And her comic timing in *Tootsie*, for example: When the phone rings after Lange's character Julie suspects Dorothy (Hoffman) is a lesbian, she picks up a baby toy in a frantic moment and puts it to her ear, thinking it's a phone, holds it there, notices her mistake, and puts it down.

In *Frances*, when she plays sixteen, her entire body becomes sixteen, with an embarrassment and bravado that tell us more about where Frances comes from than anything in the dialogue. When Frances sits in the theater with her father, squirming, her hands gradually covering her face—some of that must have come from remembering her first screening of *Kong*, but the telling quality of the gesture comes from one whose first exposure to serious acting was in silence and motion.

"His influence was profound," Jessica said. "He was my guru." The works his students learned with him were "components of thoughts," she described it, "somewhat abstract and ambiguous." Using their imaginations and their bodies, the students would create one abstract image after another. "It wasn't gymnastic," Lange said. "It could be the train of a dress of a lady-in-waiting to a queen and how it moves, a floating leaf, a bird circling, a child rising from sleep, thread unwinding. You always needed him there to create the imagery."

After work, the young people would congregate at Paris cafés and passionately discuss the day's lesson. "That's all we'd talk about," Jessica recalled. "If he complimented you, it was a great thrill, and if he did not, or worse, ignored your presence, you were crushed."

Like the others, Lange had been supplementing her meager savings with street performances, but the next spring, she was delighted to find a job with the Opéra Comique. It was essentially a walk-on part, with sixteen costume changes—but it was professional work, and included one mime piece for six entire minutes. Naturally, she couldn't tell her mentor, who scoffed at all material exposures of mime, but the job paid the rent—and allowed Lange to move to a somewhat better apartment—on the rue de Seine, several floors above the Raymond Duncan Gallery.

For the next seven months, life was pleasant, indeed. She had her paycheck, her little apartment in a charming neighborhood, her mime classes, and an intriguing circle of travelers and fellow mime devotees. She performed occasionally on the street, acted in café theater plays, and grew close to others who had made a similar voyage to study with Decroux, some of whom became lifelong friends.

It was her own life, dictated by her own passion, for the first time since she had abandoned painting and taken off with Paco. "Paco came when he could," Lange noted, with no more detail than that. The status of the marriage, less than a year old, deteriorated to these infrequent trips by Paco to Paris and Jessica's visits home for Christmas. (No good Midwestern daughter, however bohemian, misses her family's Christmas in Minnesota.)

But two years can get to be a long time away from home, even in the City of Lights. Jessie had developed a terrible cough from her damp little apartment, one which kept her hacking, she said, "like Camille or Mimi in *La Bohème*." She had grown painfully thin. And in the pages of the *International Herald Tribune,* the Watergate scandals were being daily unveiled. Lange, a Nixon-hater from day one, wanted to be home to join in on the fun of "the public humiliation of this man," as she put it. Besides, she felt, "I had been away from home long enough. The United States was where I belonged."

Two years of Decroux had been enough anyway. He apparently shared the same attitude toward his current American protégés that he'd had toward Barrault—in effect, that they should stay in the basement. Not only did Lange hide her Opéra Comique job from him, but the students grew demoralized. They'd practice pieces for six months that they knew would never see the light of day.

"He absolutely belittled any ideas of performing," Lange said. "Even in his own career, he had a disdain for public performance, a disdain for the audience, because he felt that people could never understand the meaning of his technique. So we ended up never getting out of his little studio in Boulogne. All my desires of performing onstage in mime, recording some of his most famous pieces on film, were shot down."

Even Decroux's body began to worry Lange, that she herself would end up looking as he did. "He was muscled, with big thighs. He looked like a Rodin sculpture," she remembered. "I began to feel that our bodies were beginning to look like his, big and awkward."

Not too good. Jessie decided to come back. Though there was no question about Decroux's influence, unstated and misunderstood as it would be over the following years, another route was opening up to her, to go beyond the limits of an unappreciated (at that time, anyway) art form like mime, to get out of the basement.

Acting. And that meant back to New York.

The actress as a fourth-grader: Jessica Phyllis Lange (right) in August 1958 with her friend Katherine Hedin in Sauk Centre, Minnesota, one of the eighteen small towns her family moved to throughout her childhood. A lifelong animal lover, Jessie holds her family dog while her friend poses with a puppy she just won from a local pet store. (Photograph courtesy Charlotte Hedin)

JESSE LANGE
"Jess"
Artistic, dramatic, and fun is she, a new girl Cloquet was glad to see.

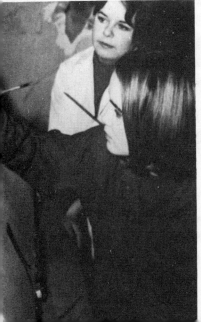

"Artist at Work," reads the caption from the Cloquet High School yearbook. A serious painter, Lange attended the University of Minnesota on a painting scholarship.

Another yearbook shot of the class of 1967. Lange's spirit of rebellion was "really percolating," she said, by her senior year in this tiny northern lumber town.

"Jessie thanks the Kiwani's" to a backdrop of the psychedelic theme she designed for the prom.

Left and below:
Lange's would-be
stage debut as the
female lead in *Rebel
Without a Cause,*
here seen in
rehearsal, was
abruptly canceled
after a fatal
stabbing occurred
in the school.
Lange was bitterly
disappointed.

An honor student,
Lange wrote for
the school paper
and would later
regret never
finishing college.

Left: Jessica Lange rests against King Kong's hand, the backdrop that the rest of the world would know her by when she was cast as Kong's love in the extravagent Dino De Laurentiis 1976 remake of the classic monster movie. The role both began and nearly ended her career. (UPI/Bettmann News Photo)

After a freewheeling youth of travel, mime, waitressing, and acting lessons, a leggy 27-year-old Jessica plays starlet for the camera around the time of the relentless publicity for *King Kong*. (Botti/Sygma)

Lange, draped in white, is Angelique, the Angel of Death, alongside co-star Roy Scheider, in real-life lover Bob Fosse's *All That Jazz* (1979), her first picture in more than two years after *Kong*. (Sygma)

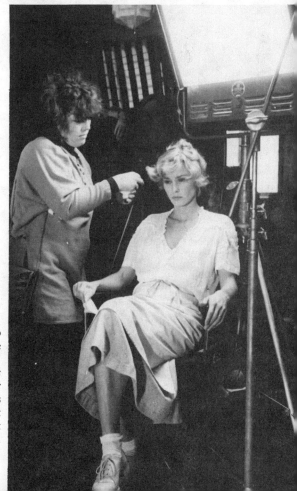

Jessica Lange visibly gets into her character of Cora, the murderous heroine of the 1981 remake of *The Postman Always Rings Twice*, while a hairdresser fusses with her locks. Lange's performance as Cora brought the 31-year-old actress her first real acclaim and turned around her career.

Every man's eyes in this picture are on Jessica, including co-star Jack Nicholson's, as extras and stars await an exterior shot for *Postman*, set in the Depression.

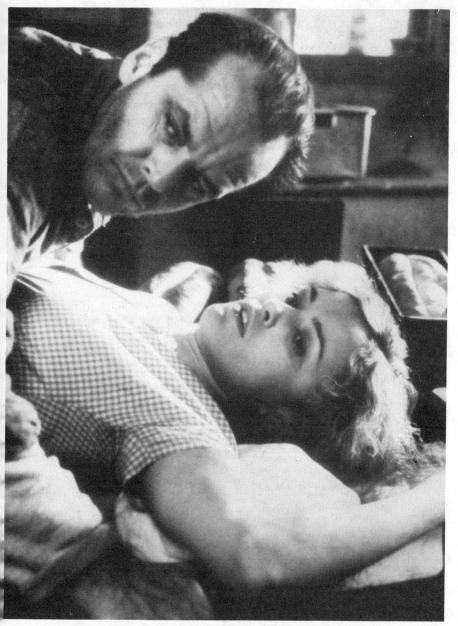

Lange and Nicholson pause for directions atop a kitchen table that was the backdrop for one of the film's torrid love scenes.

Left: Jessica Lange wheels 3-month-old Alexandra, offspring of unwedded bliss with dancer Mikhail Baryshnikov, at the Cannes Film Festival, in May of 1981, while Jack Nicholson looks on. (Laforet/Simon/Gamma)

Opposite above: A sultry Lange in Cannes in the spring of 1981, a few months after the birth of her daughter and just before filming *Frances.* (Philippe Ledru/Sygma)

Opposite below: Lange and Baryshnikov, in one of their rare photographs together, near the end of their six-year, on-again, off-again relationship, in April 1983. (Jim Frank/Gamma)

Above: Lange rages as *Frances* (1982), in a performance that won her a 1983 Oscar nomination for Best Actress. (Gamma-Liaison)

Below: Director Graeme Clifford paired Sam Shepard as onscreen lover Harry York with Jessica Lange in *Frances* because he thought they'd get along well together. He was right. (Gamma-Liaison)

Left: Lange's delectable portrait in *Tootsie* (1982) of a soap-opera star who arouses the ardor of Dustin Hoffman in drag opened the eyes of the rest of the country as well, and won her an Oscar. (Gamma-Liaison)

Below: Jessica exults at the Academy Awards in Los Angeles after capturing the 1983 Oscar for Best Supporting Actress. Lange was the first woman in forty years to be nominated in one year for both Best Actress and Best Supporting Actress.

Playing a beleaguered Iowa couple, Lange and Shepard watch their
onscreen toddler on the set of *Country* (1984), which Lange
co-produced. Her moving portrait of a struggling contemporary farm
wife brought her a second Best Actress nomination in 1985. Two years
later, she and Shepard would have their own baby girl. (Sygma)

Jessica Lange pauses during press conference duties in New York City.
(Sonya Moskowitz/Images)

Above and right: The reclusive Sam Shepard appears with his love, co-star, and co-producer at the opening night festivities for the New York Film Festival, where *Country* opened. (Doug Vann)

Right and below: Spurning the "dispensable female role," Jessica dyed her hair red and adapted a seductive drawl as Maggie in the critically acclaimed Showtime production for pay-cable of Tennessee Williams's *Cat on a Hot Tin Roof.* (Courtesy of Showtime/Mitzi Trumbo)

Brunette this time, Lange playcd the feisty, legendary country singer Patsy Cline in *Sweet Dreams* (1985) and lip-synched up a storm. Lange got raves and another Best Actress nomination. (Sygma)

8

DOING TIME IN GOTHAM

"I came home to study acting," Jessica said. But she wasn't exactly greeted with cartwheels. She sublet a fifth-floor walk-up in the West Village that lacked, among other things, a sink in the bathroom. It cost $175 a month, cracked ceiling and all. It was "a very sad place," she remembered ruefully. "That's when I decided to start modeling. It's called eating. That was exactly what it was. I had no idea what a long struggle it would be before I started to make any money at all."

"I was poor," Jessica told one interviewer frankly. "I've always been poor." The sixties were over, even if Nixon had resigned, and it was time to put passions aside and make a decent living and study her craft—acting. She signed up for one class at Herbert Berghof's studio and went knocking on model agency doors to support the lessons. Fate helped her on the finances—she had her first apartment for six months but paid rent for only two because the landlord asked for money on the spot and then never came back. Jess, broke as usual, didn't go looking for him.

Twenty-five is late to start modeling—these days, in fact, it's almost too old to model, period, and it wouldn't be surprising if the slender young woman had to lie more than once about her age. Nonetheless, her natural good looks were enough for one of New York's top agencies, Wilhelmina. Her hair was lightened. She got braces for her overbite. Her bushy, dark eyebrows were plucked and shaped. She was already skinny enough—a mere 110 pounds on a lanky five-foot seven-inch frame.

Between the modeling agency and the *King Kong* role she had no idea she would soon land, Jessica Lange was transformed from a pretty but unremarkable Midwestern college girl into the stunning blonde beauty that would define her for the next decade. It was never a transformation she was comfortable with. She hated modeling. She couldn't bear to dress up. It would take her hours to find something decent to wear, later, when she had to be seen out with Misha Baryshnikov. She even went so far as to once outline the contents of her makeup purse to a visiting reporter: a stub of shadow, some ancient mascara, a tube of lipstick so old "it's waxy." The incessant vanity of modeling annoyed her, and the rejection of people on a purely physical basis was a value she despised.

But, in the end, it was a job. It was four months before she got her first modeling work. Paris, it turned out, was an easier place to begin a modeling career, and Jessica went back for a lengthy visit, some work, and some companionship. One friend from Paris was the future star Grace Jones. And a male comrade at the time was another mime afficionado, Phillip Petit, who would gain notoriety for walking a tightrope between the two World Trade Towers in Manhattan. Not exactly a dull crowd. Antonio Lopez, the well-known fashion artist, spied Lange walking into an apartment complex in Paris that year and left a note on each door, trying to track down this unknown blonde for an ad campaign requiring a Marilyn Monroe type of model. Lange showed up two days later, and the two became good friends.

By fall of that year, having returned to New York, Lange had finally done some runway work and catalogue photos, including one cosmetic ad for Elizabeth Arden. That remained the extent of her modeling career. "There was a myth generated that I was this high-paid, top cover girl," Lange said testily to one reporter. "But that was bullshit. There were no covers." Later, when she would become a cog in the publicity machine for *King Kong*, Lange bitterly resented the "model-turned-actress" label. The *Kong* people made it seem "like the girl (herself) never had a thought in her head, and one day decided she was going to be an actress. I'd rather have been a waitress-turned-actress, a student-turned-actress, anything but not that."

At the time, however, she was only too aware of the model-turned-actress syndrome—because that was precisely what she wanted. "I kept doing it [modeling] because I saw the trend in the last ten years of models like Lauren Hutton and Ali MacGraw and Cybill Shepherd [who] had made the transition to films, and I wanted to do that, too," she said to *The New York Times* in 1976.

To this end, Lange took an evening acting class, with several professional models, from the New York acting coach Warren Robertson. Robertson found Jessica "very sensitive, very sincere, with a humility about studying acting." What Robertson remembered about Lange was "a strange quality of kind of an innocence violated. It gave her a great kind of humility and at the same time a ferocity that was the most unusual combination." Her work as a dancer and a mime added a physical sensuality, "an animal-like character that was just awesome when she was onstage." Lange impressed the class immediately, even though she was nervous and unsure of what she was doing in terms of acting. "Jessica had a tremendous emotionality, a childlikeness about her," Robertson remembered. "She had a sense of spontaneity in her work." It was in this class that Lange was introduced to the story of Frances Farmer for the first time, and several of the class's graduates went on to become successful actors.

Modeling was, in turn, supplemented by a job working nights at the Lion's Head, a dark, wood-lined bar below street level in Greenwich Village, and an institution in its own right. "I remember walking into the Lion's Head restaurant about that time and seeing this extraordinarily pretty blonde waitress," said one former actress, "and I remember someone telling me she wanted to be an actress, and I thought to myself: She'll get all the parts."

That is, if she could survive working nights at the Lion's Head. The place was a favorite for Irish-American writers who liked to get drunk and pretend they were Dylan Thomas. The brawls were "terrible, awful," Jessica reported. But, "of all the jobs I had for survival," Jessica told David Rosenthal of *New York* magazine, "it was by far the most pleasant. Something interesting was always happening. It was the pinnacle."

She was clearing the princely sum of $500 a month, more than she'd seen before in her life. Paco Grande was somewhere making documentaries. Elsewhere in Manhattan, dance audiences hailed a handsome young Soviet named Mikhail Baryshnikov as the dancer of the century after his defection in 1974 from the Soviet Union. Elsewhere in Manhattan, too, the hippest theater audiences hailed a prolific young writer, Sam Shepard, who, like Jessica, had just returned from a self-imposed exile across the Atlantic and who would move to San Francisco to pursue his theatrical work there. But while the stars of her future lovers streaked brightly across the firmament, Jessica worked and rode subways and climbed the stairs to her acting classes with a million other less stellar souls.

They shared not merely a location, but a state of mind: They were all about to make it. Like the photographers, the other actors, the writers, the poets, the friends who, like her, had returned from Paris and eked out a living, Lange was one of many for whom fame was right around the corner. You put up with the snubs, the deprivation, the lack of money, all because of a projected future, where fame waits in the wings. Years later, sitting in the Lion's Head, performance artist Marty Watt would recall: "She was this cute, beautiful girl, and then she was Jessica Lange and everyone said, 'Great, good for her,' but they kept doing whatever they were doing—they all thought they were stars anyway. Most of us still do."

Lange's rise to stardom would probably appear in the fantasy lives of many. Everyone wants it. But particularly Jessica Lange wanted it. She had gone back to Minnesota after that last visit to Paris and looked at the empty streets of Cloquet—at the Diamond Match factory, the VFW building, the pizza joints and bars where she had partied not so many years before—and thought her heart would break if she had to return there to live, failed and ordinary.

Many wish and few are chosen. But Jessica Lange happened to get it. She lucked into it. She lucked into it because she worked at the Wilhelmina Agency and one week in December of 1975 the Wilhelmina Agency got a call from the producer of a new film. They were in trouble. They needed a new unknown to play the girl with the ape. Did the agency have any models? Well, yes. As a matter of fact, they did.

9

DISCOVERED

Jessica Lange picked up her copy of *The New York Times* one morning and leafed through it. There, in the movie section, she spotted an enormous ad. KING KONG IS COMING, it read, with a picture of the giant beast. "My God, why are they going to remake that movie?" Jessica later said she thought to herself. "It wasn't any good the first time." No, the original *King Kong* was not exactly this movie fan's favorite show. When *King Kong* was on the double bill in features in movie theaters, Jessica used to walk out.

Lange's feelings about the original *King Kong* were not shared by most of the rest of the world. The 1933 *King Kong* arrived on the American psyche in the age of radio, before television, before color, and only a few years after movies had sound. It used a novel approach of models and rear projection to distort scale, and, along with films like *Dracula* and *Franken- stein* (both from 1931), became a touchstone for movie escap- ism, the classic camp horror film. People loved it irrationally and remembered it all their lives.

The flamboyant Italian producer Dino De Laurentiis got the idea to remake this cult favorite as he tried to wake his fifteen- year-old daughter one morning and caught a glimpse of a poster of the original *King Kong* over her bed.

Dino De Laurentiis produced his first film at the age of twenty in 1939 in his native Italy. With his sure eye for talent and sharp commercial sense, he helped create Italian postwar cinema by producing such films as *Bitter Rice* (1946) and the young Fellini's *La Strada* (1954) and *The Nights of Cabiria* (1956), which catapulted Fellini to international fame. Breaking off his fruitful partnership with Carlo Ponti in 1957, De Laurentiis went on to win and lose fortunes on internationally developed epics like *Waterloo* and *War and Peace,* before moving to the United States in the early seventies. Here, he again hit pay dirt with pictures like Charles Bronson in *Death Wish* and Al Pacino in *Serpico.* De Laurentiis was unusual in combining sophisticated taste with a populist instinct; fifty-six years old, he made up in bravura what he lacked in height.

Now a resident of Los Angeles, Dino De Laurentiis had big plans for his film. He wanted it to be the biggest, the best, the most colossal monster movie ever made—and a beautiful love story, to boot, of Beauty and the Beast.

No one took De Laurentiis's remake idea seriously in Hollywood—until *Jaws* made $200 million dollars for Universal in 1975. Suddenly oversized, mechanical monsters were in. Paramount Pictures agreed to do the film, but since Universal was threatening to do their own *Kong* remake, De Laurentiis went out on a limb and promised to deliver *Kong* to Paramount in time for Christmas 1976. He had to fight Universal in court to substantiate his claim to the rights to RKO's story.

Years before, buried in the side streets of small, unknown Midwestern towns, Jessie Lange would while away the hours playing scenes to herself from *Gone With the Wind.* Ironically, her rise from unknown to screen star could have rivaled Vivian Leigh's as Scarlett. The legend was the same: A powerful producer, hunting a new fresh face for a famous role, plucks a young woman from obscurity after a nationwide search. Like David Selznick (who had also produced the 1933 *King Kong*), De Laurentiis hoped to generate publicity by his search, but, also like Selznick, he found the right unknown eluding him, despite tryouts of scores of girls. The second week in December, a frustrated and slightly panicky director and producer sent out calls to New York's modeling agencies to send them some new unknown faces for the girl creature, inexplicably named Dwan.

"The woman in the television department [at Wilhelmina] suggested that I go out to test," Jessica recalled. "She told them I had studied acting and that I was serious." Knowing her own lowly status as a model, Lange was surprised to suddenly find herself in the position of would-be starlet. "They didn't know who to send."

She got the call on Monday, December 17, and was told to pack her bags and leave that night for Los Angeles. It was like something out of a daydream—a Hollywood audition? Who cared what the movie was! Jessie started throwing things into a suitcase. If nothing else, it was a free trip to California. She could drive down and see her sister Jane and her niece living on their sailboat in San Diego. Maybe she could even rewrite the return ticket to pay for a stopover visit in Minneapolis, just in time for Christmas. Couldn't hurt.

Jessica waited by the phone all day for a call that didn't come. Any would-be actress has the little speeches on file for the particular torture known as waiting for an audition. Jessica repeated them to herself that night: Lots of people come to New York to do preliminary casting and nothing usually comes of it.

But the next morning, the phone jangled her awake. Her agent told her she had two hours to make her plane to Los Angeles. A car arrived to whisk her to the airport. "It was the first time," Jessica noted with some precision later, in 1977, "that I had ever ridden in a limousine."

Hollywood, Hollywood. There is no place like it, and no feeling quite like the first time a virgin dreamer sets foot in the factory town of dreams. You leave the barren haunts of New York and Minnesota behind and find yourself whizzing down Sunset Boulevard, past palm trees and white limousines. Hollywood—it really exists! That first time is a little like Dorothy stepping from black and white into the Technicolor world of Oz. Lange and another model who made the trip with her were deposited at the exclusive Beverly Wilshire Hotel, unquestionably the most luxurious environs Jessica had ever seen, let alone lived in. A doorman in a top hat took their bags.

"It was really Hollywood. We had arrived. It was all so splendid," Jessica remembered. No spurning of the tinsel and its glory for Jessica Lange at twenty-six, fresh from working nights at the Lion's Head. This was a ticket, a way out. Naturally, Jessica had assumed, with some dignity, that she would make it in New York as an actress. But this would do.

Jessica sat at the Beverly Wilshire for four entire days—not the worst fate in the world, if the alternative is a frigid New York City. Paramount sent over the script. She got out a pencil and got to work.

Only a few short years before, trips to California were made on interstate freeways, sleeping in the backs of vans, crashing on friends' floors. Not so today. Jess could have eaten for a day in Paris on the price of a glass of orange juice at the Wilshire. Living off room service, staying in her room, Jessica studied the script, remembering all the things she'd been learning in two years of mime and another two of acting classes. She began to think that this was going to be a good movie, after all, as she studied the script that De Laurentiis had been working on with writer Lorenzo Semple Jr. for the last six months. The only thing she disagreed with was that the role of the girl was "a little too campy." "I didn't know what they had in mind," she said. "In fact, nobody did. They didn't either."

The twenty-six-year-old novice had seen at a glance the problem with the film. It wasn't camp. It wasn't a farce, but it wasn't real tragedy, either—and it wasn't even that scary, since even a remade *Kong* was, by now, a familiar character, almost loveable. It lacked any clear focus as either comedy or suspense—it became a role and a movie that no one took seriously.

But at the moment director John Guillermin and the producers took the part and the movie very seriously indeed. While Jessica made long-distance phone calls and planned her weekend with her sister, another familiar Hollywood scene was taking place over at Paramount Studios. Dino was furious. He and the executive producer—his twenty-four-year-old son —were ready to send the two models "right back home on the plane," her agent told Lange later. Dino knew one thing about the part, and that was that he didn't want this Jessica Lange person. "The first time I looked at her, I said to myself: terrible. Here is a girl with nothing at all. I didn't want to make a test." Dino and his son conducted some screaming matches on the phone with the Wilhelmina Agency. What was the idea of sending them skinny, colorless New York models? For Christ sake, they fumed, that Lange girl has braces on her teeth. "The key was I wasn't pretty enough," Jessica later said with a grin.

This assessment was a common comment about Jessica Lange in her first few years in acting. One Hollywood director who met a dark-haired Jessica and her crowd when she was in Paris in her earlier, starving-artist days, recalls: "She was nothing to look at." Reporters interviewing her during and after the production of *King Kong* would note in passing how she really didn't look very pretty, very much like a movie star, when they met her in person.

But—the big *but*—give this woman a role to play, a camera to play to, and something happens—to her, and to her audience, whoever that may be. When Jessica finally got to her audition at Paramount on Friday morning, that audience consisted of six other models, moving on and off a temporary jungle stage like so many dolls on an assembly line. Jessica wasn't scared. She was so convinced nothing could happen that she didn't take it all that seriously. It was a terrific experience, she thought, coming in to do a screen test, "but I didn't have any fantasies."

Even without the fantasies, the scene was "really demoralizing," she remembered. Guillermin, the British director (*Towering Inferno*), wasn't even on the set. The second unit director and a couple of electricians and cameramen looked on, preeminently bored, as yet another blonde model was dressed in a T-shirt and cutoffs and took her place on a bed. Lange looked warily at a pillow tied on one post, meant to represent Kong. She began thinking about the scene, which was to be where Dwan wakes up and finds she's been rescued. As she headed for the bed, she got herself ready: discovery, rescue. What are the feelings, the gestures? She got into the bed, prepared to do her first Hollywood screen test—and the crew broke for lunch.

Jessica sat there, alone on the set, feeling like that level of nobody that exists only in Hollywood. Finally, the crew returned—Guillermin with them, this time—and she began to act.

She did the scene once. Then again. And again. "It stopped being a test, and he started to direct me. Then I went on to do a second scene. There had been only two girls who had moved to a second scene." Guillermin sent the call to Dino to get himself down there—"This girl has something sensational!" Dino found this hard to believe.

By this time, Jessica was on her third scene. And Dino changed his mind. "Amazing," Dino said to himself. "This girl in front of the camera, she's so fantastic. Dino, you were wrong."

That's not quite what Dino said to his unknown starlet, sitting in her dressing room, uncertain of what was happening. He pushed open the dressing room door and barged in "in his inimitable style," as Lange remembered it, barking orders about improving this "girl who had nothing." At five feet seven inches, Jessica towered over the five-foot-four Dino, but he was the boss. "You have to put on weight!" he exclaimed. "You must lighten your hair. The braces must come off!" He even asked her if she wanted to have her "little boxer's nose" fixed. But Jessica wasn't worried about that. She had done it. Even the bored union crew, back from their lunch, could see something was finally happening.

Friday night, Jessica departed the luxurious confines of the Beverly Wilshire and returned to the more familiar, laid-back approach to life on her sister's thirty-foot sailboat, which she shared with her boyfriend and her seven-year-old daughter. By now, of course, she was happy to have family at what was becoming a fairly nerve-wracking time. There's nothing like a sister to help wait out life's decisions. "I still didn't believe it," Jessica said. "There were so many factors involved. I still wasn't physically right for the part."

She figured it would be awhile before Dino made up his mind, but when the two girls called home that Sunday, their mother in Minnesota told them that a Mr. De Laurentiis had been calling all over the country for Jessie. Well. This, as they say in the business, was it.

When Jessica got back to Los Angeles Monday morning, Dino greeted her with a contract that she "had to sign by five o'clock or I wouldn't get the part." True to Dino's old-fashioned movie mogul demeanor, getting a lawyer or agent to represent her, 1975 or no 1975, was not even mentioned. But it was a contract in six figures for seven years, meaning more money than anyone she had ever known had earned. Jessica put her signature on a seven-year contract. "By five o'clock that afternoon," Jessica said the next year, "I had signed away my life for seven years and was on a plane for Minnesota." Time for Christmas.

By the lights of the Christmas tree, Jessica showed her parents the contract. It was a happy time in the Lange family. Jessie's good news shared the spotlight with eldest sister Ann's announcement that she was pregnant with her first child. Her grandma asked Jessie if she was going to be able to see the movie on television. Jessica said she doubted it, that it wouldn't be on television for a long, long time.

10

KING KONG

Jessica Lange stopped answering questions from interviewers about *King Kong* in 1981, shortly after her critically acclaimed performance in *The Postman Always Rings Twice*. She's refused to answer in the reams of interviews she's done since. When *Kong* came out, Lange offered the prediction that she would never be remembered for her role in *King Kong*, that it would always be associated with Fay Wray and this has turned out, at long last, to be true. Very few people do remember her in *King Kong*. Most people forgot she had the part at all.

But that part hung around her neck like a noose for years. In every interview, all through the relationship with Baryshnikov, when she was known in the trades as Jessica *(King Kong)* Lange, until she finally stopped answering questions about it. "I have nothing more to say on that subject," she told *Life* in 1982. "It bores me silly."

One quick glance at the publicity material for *King Kong* and one understands why. Jessica Lange, "a topflight model," found her "dream come true" when she landed "the most sought-after part in years." "Not since the days of Marilyn Monroe and Kim Novak has Hollywood seen the creation of an important female star, a process now happening to Jessica

Lange." Process is right. Jessica became a platinum blonde. She gained twenty-five pounds.

"Jessica," read the press material, "lived up to expectations when she made her first public appearance held aloft in the hand of King Kong." At a jammed press conference, she sat in the hastily constructed Kong hand, while a hundred shutters snapped. One thinks of Cecil B. DeMille's famous line in *Sunset Boulevard*, "A dozen press agents working overtime can do terrible things to the human spirit."

Jessica spent New Year's Eve alone in the Beverly Wilshire, which was already beginning to lose a little of its glamour. It was the last serenity she would know for a long, long time. With two weeks to go before shooting began, she found a Brentwood cottage to rent in the Pacific Palisades, a block from the ocean. She moved in some plants, her copy of *I Ching*, records, and her black Scottie, Jake. Costume fittings and makeup tests began immediately. A press conference was arranged to introduce the one human star of the picture.

The situation was chaos. There was no Kong to speak of. Not merely no mechanically constructed Kong; there wasn't even a clear vision in Dino's and the others' heads of what Kong should be like. There was no more than a scant three weeks' worth of shooting before a Kong would be needed—but at least four months of preproduction were needed, De Laurentiis himself admitted to the press.

He told them shooting would begin January 15. This rush schedule took its toll on everyone involved—the director John Guillermin, who inherited an ill-conceived and unready project that he was supposed to turn into a mega-monster movie, the special effects people, and, of course, their star. (Dino's first choice for director, Roman Polanski, refused on the grounds that he didn't know what to do with the ape.)

103

The Italian designer Rambaldi had been commissioned by De Laurentiis to design the ape. In the sea of confusion about what Kong should look like, Rambaldi cleverly offered sketches of the girl in Kong's hand. The right proportion of girl to ape grip then decided the rest of the animal's proportions. Unfortunately, the drawing that Dino and Guillermin liked best meant that Kong would be about forty feet tall. Makeup wizard Rick Baker—who happened to be a gorilla nut, a student of their movements for years—became the live, six-foot-scale version.

Fifteen technicians working overtime for thirteen weeks managed to make the mechanical portions of Kong from Rambaldi's sketches. (Rambaldi himself spoke no English and simply deposited his drawings with the special effects unit under Glen Robinson, who did not appreciate being ordered about in Italian.) Twelve tons of hydraulic pipes and electronically controlled levers, this giant mechanical Kong made impressive publicity material himself, but continually broke down, and never did learn how to walk. It was the same with everything else.

"Nothing was ever ready," Lange said. "The sets weren't ready. Kong wasn't ready. Everybody was winging it." Including, of course, Jessie herself. The new Marilyn Monroe was so inexperienced that in her first scenes, she didn't know what was meant by "hitting her marks"—the spots where an actor has to arrive to be in the correct position for the camera. Her co-stars, Jeff Bridges and Charles Grodin, helped her out. Charles Grodin, then forty and supplementing a successful career in New York theater with occasional forays to Hollywood, would become a lifelong friend.

The plot of the 1976 *King Kong*, which tried to be faithful to the original while updating it, described an oil tanker on its

way to an unexplored island, shrouded in clouds, which supposedly housed a limitless oil supply. En route, they pick up
a stranded would-be actress, Dwan. On board are a scientist,
played by Jeff Bridges, and an oil engineer, played by Charles
Grodin, along with various other members of the huge oil
conglomerate out to claim this island's oil. Kong is discovered
on the island, and Dwan is offered to him as a sacrifice by the
natives. She manages to calm the angry beast and is eventually
rescued; Kong is captured and put in the hold of the oil tanker
to be brought back to the United States. Once there, of course,
the infuriated Kong breaks loose for the obligatory raging-
through-Manhattan scene, which ends with him atop the
World Trade Towers. Dwan and the scientist have tried, and
failed, to stop all this, but in the end only see Kong surrounded
by throngs of people, lying dead in front of the World Trade
Center.

Most of this was to be shot on location in New York and on
Kauii, a remote island in Hawaii where, according to Dino, no
film crew had gone before. The hundred-plus crew arrived on
the island in March, to the distress of a honeymooning couple,
who thought they'd found a private paradise retreat!

Big break or no big break, this film had some obvious drawbacks—obvious, that is, when Jessica got to the set and realized
she was supposed to be held aloft forty feet in the air by a crane,
in a hand operated by five mechanics by remote control. When
the stunt girl tested the arm, a cable broke and she dropped to
the ground. Another stunt girl was nearly crushed by the
fingers when one mechanic got his instructions wrong. And
Jessica herself got a searing pinched nerve when the mechanics
misjudged a movement and a tap on the head from Kong's
hand nearly knocked her out. As an essentially reasonable
person, Jessica was terrified of the physical aspects of this job.

But she did them. Over and over. Trying to act natural in a mechanical hand forty feet in the air. Even when it wasn't scary, it was just plain uncomfortable.

But there was something even harder than overcoming fear of bodily harm. Movie audiences would think of Lange, this blonde nothing, as having the hilarious job of playing to an ape. But even an ape would have been preferable to what she did act to—which *was* nothing.

For three months inside the MGM studio, she ran around in a little bikini outfit and grass skirt, and played out her emotions to a bare spot on the wall where Kong's head would be in the finished scene. "It was really lonely," she told Judy Klemesrud of *The New York Times*. "I never saw another actor, and since the rest of the ape wasn't there, there was no real Kong to react to. I had to play to the ceiling, or to the wall, or to the floor."

In *Postman* and in *Frances*, one of Lange's outstanding characteristics is that she is, literally, so outstanding—overwhelming to the point of leaving fellow actors in the dust. Her portrayals, her women, seem to exist in a world of their own. Though she is as quick as most of her admirers to toss any references to *Kong* straight into the trash bin, one suspects that it is precisely here, in *Kong*, where Lange developed her propensity for navigating her way through a character with her own bare face.

Fantasy, substitution, personalization—these were her techniques. Mime, rather than a more naturalistic, ensemble-based form of acting, was her touchstone for the recreation of reality, giving her acting a physicality, a visceral presence even in this bimbo role.

Lange made the mistake of telling interviewers for *Time* magazine that she got "very close to the guys who worked the hand," and that "eventually, Kong became completely believable to me." This was presented in *People, Time,* and other publications as a revelation of Lange's own bimbo status—how can anyone react to a mechanical hand? To a laughable, stupid, giant fake ape?

And yet she did. What else was she supposed to do? It was her job. And the frustrating thing is that the film was so damn humorless. With every potential for real comedy, Lange had to instead play Ophelia to a hairy Hamlet.

Director John Guillermin, though workmanlike, was working on a "razor's edge," he said, between the two unwanted poles of farce and tragedy. Stepping around the edges of tact, Lange told an interviewer that John Guillermin was "very intense, not easy to categorize," and subject to "violent mood swings." The suave, British-born director would lose twenty pounds in the ragged course of the eight-month shoot. On the bright side, Guillermin, whose specialties were epic disaster flicks, rarely went over four takes for a scene. The unknown actress was the least of his problems, for the film was a budgetary Kong of its own, floundering under every imaginable problem.

Finally, the crew dismantled Kong and drove him cross-country to New York City for the final scenes of the film. Reid Rosevelt, later a New York film publicist for Orion Pictures, was working as an extra on the set of *King Kong* when the film completed its climactic wrapping-up scenes at the World Trade Center and other locations. "She was absolutely great on the set of *King Kong,*" he remembers. "There were forty thousand people and she was totally playing her scene in the middle of all this madness. She was convincing and impressive."

The final scene of the film was Lange's climactic moment—she stands in a white dress by the fallen ape, helpless to have saved him and yet powerful enough to have ruined him. By police counts, twenty thousand people showed up for this scene when word spread that De Laurentiis was shooting the scene at the World Trade Center. No one associated with the film, apparently, was prepared for the magnitude of the turn-out. Thousands of people milled around all day. Finally Guillermin grabbed the bullhorn and said: "Okay—everyone look to your left." All looked. Guillermin shouted "Cut." And that was the scene.

Later, De Laurentiis's publicity people told the press that Jessica "actually cried" during the filming of the death scene of *Kong*—a comment which drove Jessica to exasperation. "I was supposed to cry!" she said to a columnist. "Look at the script!" Nonetheless, she told a *New York Times* reporter that this was her "favorite scene." "I really loved New York," she gushed in a piece that appeared opening week in December, "and when those thousands of thousands of New Yorkers showed up and became involved in the filming, it was really exhilarating."

11

POST-*KONG*

When you're poor, you don't read the fine print, and Jessica Lange hadn't looked too closely at the publicity-tour requirement written into her *King Kong* role. "I didn't realize it would be so extensive when they said something about a promotional tour," an exhausted, flu-ridden Lange told a reporter in an interview at the end of filming when she was holed up in a Pierre Hotel suite. No sooner, it seemed, had shooting finished, than her six-week tour had begun. (De Laurentiis sent her on a $6,000 New York shopping spree when she told him she had "nothing to wear" for the tour.) She managed to stop off in the October woods of Wisconsin for a brief vacation at Lake Nebagomen—but even there, *Time* magazine sent a photographer and reporter for the massive cover story they were preparing. They snapped a photo of Jessie sitting at her parents' table, her arms on a plastic table-cloth, a cup of coffee beside her. She smoked her pack of Marlboro Lights, played with Ann's new baby, her niece and namesake, then was whisked off on a tour embracing three continents and thirty-one cities.

And on October 25, she was on the cover of *Time.* In Kong's hand. No wonder she stopped giving interviews on the subject. Many people dream of being on the cover of *Time* magazine, but hardly anyone dreams of it being in beads and bikini, squirming in the hairy black palm of a forty-foot ape.

The film was booked into one thousand theaters on the same day—one of the largest initial releases for a film at the time in North America. The merchandising tie-ins ranged from Schrafft's candy to Slurpee soda, Sedgefield blue jeans to Jim Beam bourbon.

But, in one of those rare moments of collective integrity by the American filmgoing public, the movie was a bomb, anyway. No amount of oversized Italian hype could disguise a fundamentally unthrilling, unscary, and unimpressive *Kong*.

Her friends in New York saw it and guffawed, or shrugged, or winced, or thought it was some other Jessica Lange. All her family knew was that Jessie was earning more money than all of her relatives and immediate family put together. For this once-shy child, buried in a family of four kids, it was more attention than she'd ever gotten in her life. Six weeks. Six weeks of hundreds of interviews. In an "If this is Tuesday, it must be Belgium" frame of mind, the tour began with a cross-country blitzkrieg of talk shows and interviews for newspapers —as many as four local TV shows each day, ten or twelve interviews a day in all. In Massachusetts, she gave Governor Dukakis a two-foot polyresin Kong; in Japan, she took geisha lessons. The questions were always, maddeningly, the same. It was an almost grotesque charicature of the genuine superstardom that she would have later—the difference being that, in later years, she could at least present a more realistic image of herself. The earlier experience may even explain the near-confessional nature of her interviews after such films as *Postman* and *Frances*.

But in this bout with the complex monster fame, she got to

tell a thousand different interviewers what it was like to make the film. What it was like to play to this huge ape. What it was like being Fay Wray. After the United States came Europe, Japan, back to Europe. Back in the United States, through the South, back to New York, sitting in the Pierre Hotel, wearing a white cowl-necked sweater "with a hole under the left armpit," as the *New York Times* reporter precisely observed.

Dino De Laurentiis had rewritten her past into his vision of a starlet discovered. The person he invented had very little to do with who Jessie thought herself to be, or with any of the things she'd done. Painting, mime—these were mentioned in passing, if at all, in the reams of publicity material. Paco was deliberately kept out of the picture.

Paco was in Jamaica, filming a documentary on reggae music. It was just as well. Starlets aren't supposed to be married. The publicity material didn't mention the hippie husband, and, in all of the publicity for *Kong*, no one ever printed a photograph of the two of them; Jessica was always referred to as Miss Lange.

Her future consisted of a contract with De Laurentiis. The present was the biggest movie of all time: *King Kong*. "I got clear messages to look at the positive side," Lange said. At night, she sat alone, exhausted, making long-distance phone calls to friends, staring at another empty wall—this time in a hotel room in God knows where.

At the end of six weeks, she went home to Wisconsin with the flu. This was not what fame was supposed to be about.

Quiet is a visceral pleasure of the north Wisconsin woods. When you arrive from the big cities of the world, it is the quiet that relaxes you, with a sort of natural massage of sound, from the pine trees and heavy snow to your ears and into your troubled mind. It is the thing that separates these northern woods from the frenetic sounds and fury of the rest of the planet. For a Midwestern girl, this is home.

And home had never looked better. "They'll probably have to put me in a rest home," Lange had told her *Washington Post* interviewer. The Langes gathered for the Christmas they always had. Some of the more thoughtful may have paused momentarily, a plate of cookies in their hand, on their way from the kitchen, to see if they felt any differently about their Jess now that she was famous—and realized that they didn't, she was still the same, only blonder. Paco arrived for a rare visit, one that did nothing to solidify a relationship that had had no visible physical unity for more than five years.

The status of her marriage with Paco was a mystery for most journalists covering the *King Kong* story. To be divorced, to have a lover, all that was fine—but to be married to someone and then simply leave and not bother to get divorced seemed like the kind of thing only spacey chicks did in silly movies about the sixties. Clearly she was her own woman, romantically. At the end of a tour, she "giggled nervously," according to her rather cynical interviewer Jan Hodenfield (and who wouldn't be? he's only interviewing the girl who played Fay Wray in *King Kong*): "It's not as though we're separated or anything or considering being divorced, it's just that he has his career, which doesn't change because mine has gone in another direction." Something of an understatement, in retrospect. "And I've never hesitated from doing anything that I've wanted to do," she concluded. "Paco was really happy for me when all this happened. But his life hasn't changed because of it. He still does what he wants to do, and I do what I want to do."

After the rest of the family had gone back to work, Jessica sat by the lake and looked at the ice fishermen and the snow and the trees. "It was heavenly . . . it really was, it was so quiet," she said. She played some more with her sister's baby, Jessica. Soon she had to go back to Los Angeles. Soon she had to decide on the next step. Soon she had to go back to being— what? An actress? A starlet? Certainly not a model . . .

Everyone makes a big deal of midlife crises, but it's the failures of the late twenties that can really do you in. Just when you think life is supposed to fall into place, it does the opposite. Lange had zoomed onto a fast track that she hardly knew existed a year before. Now she was twenty-seven and a has-been. A cover article in *People* magazine, "Getting the Monkey Off Her Back," did nothing to separate her image from the *Kong* role—they had a grinning Kong face on the cover behind her! Hers was the quintessential post-Warhol celebrity-hood—a fifteen-minute burst of superstardom that lasted for December of 1976. The film did not lose money—De Laurentiis had seen to it that tie-in promotions and sales of overseas rights covered the bottom line—but, grossing $80 million over the Christmas season, it did nowhere near what was expected of it at the box office. It was certainly not another *Jaws*.

One magazine she happened to pick up after the tour, *New West*, had called her performance "one-dimensional." One-dimensional? After all that work? "It made me wonder if all the work was worth it," she said. The bad reviews hurt—and the picture was a field day for reviewers, for whom trashing a really terrible, highly touted, overbudget film restores a sense of personal mission. "There's only one way to do it [Kong] and it's been done," Vincent Canby wrote.

It was some comfort, but not much, that a few brief paragraphs nestled in these scathing reviews of *Kong* praised her performance. Pauline Kael responded to Lange's "fast yet dreamy comic style," and wrote, "you like her, the way audiences liked Carole Lombard." Other reviewers compared her favorably to Eva Marie Saint and, inevitably, Marilyn Monroe. "Lange does a sort of muted Marilyn Monroe imitation in these scenes," wrote *Time* magazine in its cover story, "but there is an underlying quickness and humor in her characterization."

What now? Modeling was out, absolutely out. For one thing, she had seen the stigma placed on models by the acting community. "It's a business where you're a one-dimensional facade," Lange had said in one interview. "Only a rare few, like Lauren Hutton, have that certain something to transcend just being a physical commodity." Besides, not only was she terrible at it, but she had started modeling quite late. At twenty-seven, she was too old to be a model anymore anyway.

And Lange became depressed about what people said about her, about what she appeared to be. "The film was a joke," she realized. "And because I was the central character, I was sort of a joke." No one thought of her as an adventurer—which is really the best description of what she'd been to that point, including her acting in *Kong*. No one called her an artist, even a serious actress. Some magazine quoted Dino, of all people, calling her the next Marilyn Monroe. "That really upsets me," Lange made a point of telling a *Time* reporter within a few weeks. She didn't want to be compared to "a tragic figure who led a tragic life, who wasn't taken as the serious artist she was." The last thing she wanted was to be the next Marilyn Monroe —what could be a more terrifying fate? "I don't want to compete with her memory, to compete with anyone," Lange stressed. "I feel it's unjust to compare us."

At least she got no pressure from her parents. Father Al, himself the veteran of a dozen or more defeats on smaller, but no less wrenching, battlefields, knew the story well. "It's nothing new, happens all the time," Al Lange said. "I told her, don't let it bother you. This is what life is about, a part of the game." With the matter-of-fact wisdom that he'd required in leading a life that few could consider much more than a haphazard series of failures, Al Lange pointed out something that the rest of us are likely to forget as well: "With most people, when they get knocked down, you don't hear all about it. You know, a farmer doesn't make a wheat sale, a lawyer doesn't pass the bar exam—happens all the time with no to-do. But in Hollywood it's a big issue. It wouldn't have bothered me if she hadn't gone back after that."

Things weren't too clear in the love department either. Paco was home for a part of the holidays. The marriage was clearly on iffy turf. She went so far as to tell *People* magazine in January that the situation "was difficult."

In January, Jessica returned uncertainly to her apartment a block from the Pacific with her black Scottie Jake, put on Schubert records, and waited for the phone to ring. It didn't. "All this attention that had been showered on me for a year was cut off cold," Lange said much later. "Because I didn't know any better, I didn't know that it had all been strictly business. I thought they liked me! It was a rude awakening." Her self-doubt grew.

She would not, she said firmly, do a sequel to *King Kong*—"I want Dino to see that in print," she told one reporter in October, before the film was released. "Artistically," she said pointedly, relying on understatement, "there is nothing else to do with that." Fortunately, the film's lackluster performance spared her of that gagging prospect. And, of course, she was being paid handsomely to do nothing. The idea was to make another film.

For a time, Jessica did manage to hire a manager for herself, one Mike Rosenfield, who gushed about her potential. Jessica's second picture, everyone agreed, was the clincher. "When you get a first opportunity like this, you have to be very careful so the Fay Wray syndrome doesn't happen," Rosenfield said. In other words, everyone was waiting for Jessica Lange to fall on her face. And for two years, she very nearly obliged them.

Projects did not materialize overnight, and Jessica didn't know what to do with the ones that did. By January, she had ten scripts from various places, including another De Laurentiis remake, this one of the 1937 classic *Hurricane,* a part eventually cast with Mia Farrow. "There has been nothing that is comedy," Jessica complained, "which is too bad, because I would like to do comedy, at least for the next film." Besides, word had gotten around Hollywood that Jessica had been less than stalwart on her publicity tour. Friends from *Kong* like Charles Grodin still called her up—she didn't even have an answering service, let alone a publicist, he remembers.

One of the very few nice things that came out of that year was a letter from Bob Fosse, the hot director and choreographer of *Cabaret,* among other works, who had just won an Oscar, an Emmy, and a Tony all in the same year. "You're good," he told her—and he really thought so. He noted the sexual allure in Lange's Dwan, the intelligence struggling to break free of the silly writing. Fosse said he was planning his magnum opus, a film extravaganza based on his own life. He sent her the script in the fall of 1976. At that point, it had no part, precisely, for Lange in it, and the film was delayed for a number of reasons as Fosse rewrote it completely over the next two years.

Hiding out in Los Angeles, "where I knew cars better than I knew people," Jessica grew more and more depressed with each passing week. She felt like a failure. Only a few short years ago she had been turning her life inside out to find—what was it? oh, yes—commitment. Now all she could do was flip forlornly through the trade papers, thinking that everyone was working but she. Years later, Lange would look back and say, "The experience of *Kong* still leaves me with mixed feelings. It's too bad. . . . "

"I don't regret doing it," she would say, "but I don't like what happened afterwards." She had been "naive . . . I was not emotionally prepared for what this film would do to me. It brought me pain for some time. For a while, I lost control over my own life."

It was a case, really, of not going home again. Not home as a place, or retreat, but home as a familiar, earlier state of mind. *Kong* had plucked this waitress/actress/model from her obscurity in downtown Manhattan, a world at least self-contained, where goals were clear because they were so clearly impossible to reach.

Jessica belonged to a new order, now—to Hollywood—coincidentally named after a location, but also a state of mind, really an international set of expectations, with a bitchy etiquette and a hierarchical stratification to rival the Sun King's court.

She was little more than jester in this court—and yet she couldn't leave. The buildup as Kong's love was inexorable. Her entry was too complete—her desire to make her own dreams real, too encompassing. This was, after all, what she wanted—or what she thought it was going to lead to: money, recognition, an art. And, in the end, that's just what it did lead to. Jessica Lange, for all the harm, embarrassment, and other defects of her debut role, in the long run forged a serious career out of a very highly publicized bimbohood. She absolutely maximized what she could have gotten from that part.

12

BACK TO NEW YORK

T he members of certain preliterate tribes won't allow photographs to be taken of them. In the image of the face, they believe, lies the soul—to take a picture of that face is to steal the soul away. Selling one's face in America is not the same thing as selling one's soul—not quite. If you are blonde and a waitress at the Lion's Head and no one in your family has ever had any money and you take a part in what promises to be one of the biggest pictures of this or any other year and get a seven-year, six-figure income for it, that is not quite the same thing as selling your soul.

But to anyone else, it looked pretty damn close to it. It looked worse—as if there weren't a soul to sell. It can't be a coincidence, then, that the former Fay Wray has gone on to make serious, powerful—in fact, despairing—films when given the first opportunity. Everyone else has forgotten *King Kong* by now, but one doesn't forget, oneself, the things that had to be sold to get one where one needed—needed, and passionately wanted—to be. Those debts stay etched in one's own memory long after they erode from everyone else's.

It is difficult for the public who knows Jessica Lange as the tour-de-force actress of *Frances*, the stunning charmer of *Tootsie*, and the stoic, politicized actress-producer of *Country* to recall how low her status was in the two years following *King Kong*.

Lange has never spoken publicly against De Laurentiis about this period, but much of the problem with her career stemmed from that hastily signed contract, which gave De Laurentiis final approval over all films she wanted to make. Exactly why none was approved is hard to say. (The contract was canceled by mutual consent in 1980.)

It was, she told Julia Cameron of *American Film*, "a bad period." The marriage to Paco was clearly over. The answer, once again, was to go back to New York. "A couple of months in L.A., and I immediately knew that if we were talking self-preservation, we were talking moving back to New York," Jessica said. Back to the noise and the dirt and the tiny apartment and the two-hour drives to anyplace peaceful. Back with Jake, the black Scottie, a new wardrobe, and a steady, if unearned, paycheck. Good-bye to the publicist. Hello, acting. When in doubt, take another acting class. Lange resumed her acting classes with renewed fervor.

"I had to get into introverted self-examination to get rid of the self-doubts that began to appear," Lange said. "I restructured everything. I didn't work for two years." Later, she would be proud that she survived this episode without benefit of a therapist's couch. One suspects her precisely spat denunciation of the hospital psychiatrist in *Frances* may come from her own feelings about the profession.

What was needed, clearly, she decided, was a touch of class. That, in fact, was about the only permanent gift she got from the multimillionaire. She was put on De Laurentiis's social list from the moment she got the part—wined and dined, introduced to the best. Including the best of one sort in particular —the best dancer in the world. Mikhail Baryshnikov.

She found a new, sunny, one-bedroom apartment in the fashionable East Side, off Park Avenue, a vast improvement on the old downtown digs. Misha Baryshnikov, it so happened, lived in a friend's penthouse some twenty blocks uptown, at 581 Fifth Avenue.

One observer reports that Jessica Lange was poring over *People* magazine articles about Baryshnikov during time off from *Kong* shoots in her cottage in Hawaii—a crush on the ineffably cute Misha already in ripe development. She had, reportedly, already met him early in the shooting of *King Kong*. Ironically, their spurts to fame occurred almost simultaneously, though Baryshnikov's, of course, was on a far different plane. Back to back in the *Time* magazine of December of 1976 are reviews of Baryshnikov's *Nutcracker Suite* on television and Lange in *King Kong*! In the meantime, both were making their film debuts—he in *The Turning Point*—that very spring in Hollywood.

When Misha noticed the blonde actress at a post-*Kong* party in Los Angeles and asked who she was, someone told him she was King Kong's girlfriend. Whereupon he asked, innocently enough, "Who's King Kong? Can I meet him?"

Misha had a few things to learn about American culture. In fact, his English was still on the rocky side; he and Jessica conversed in French. By the time *The Turning Point* had finished its principal photography, the two of them were well-acquainted enough to attend the wrap party together.

It may have seemed like unlikely pairing, but it was more like strangers in a strange land—Cloquet, Minnesota, and Moscow are parallel in latitude (actually, Minneapolis is a colder city than Moscow) and psychologically about equidistant from Hollywood as well. And, as Paco had once seemed exotic, new, representing a higher level of knowledge, so too did this brilliant dancer. But it would be quite a while before she had any claims on this lover. Quite a while indeed. It wasn't until the fall of 1979 that Jessica's name was linked with Misha's in national publications such as a *People* magazine story of the nation's ten most eligible men. When, around that time, it became clear that King Kong's girlfriend was now Misha's, "her stock really went up," remembers one observer who covered the New York dance scene. "Everyone thought she was a bimbo, but she had to have some smarts to go out with Misha, because he was so smart."

The down side was that he was a genius and she was a nobody. From a Paul Taylor dancer: "I can't forget the time Misha came into rehearsal and helped me into one of those Paul Taylor lifts—you know, the kind in which the woman stands on the front of the man's thighs. I got up there and looked down at Misha's body. I felt the energy in his arms and hands and the feeling of the strength in his muscles. I almost collapsed. His body is like liquid gold. I can't explain it. I felt so much compassion and respect—a kind of love for him." Pretty rough competition.

"I was going with the greatest dancer of the century," Lange told *American Film*'s Cameron. "Misha was being courted by kings. One night at dinner with what was the Greek aristocracy, this man leaned over across me and said to Misha, 'I see you travel with your secretary.' I thought: Either I shouldn't be in this relationship or I'm going to have to find a way to shut these people out." Lange's obsessive privacy about this obviously superstar match probably stems from this. Interestingly, once she achieved some status of her own, beginning with *Postman*, she began to be photographed with him at charitable events and so forth, even going so far as to appear in *People* magazine, in "Life With Baryshnikov and Baby," to publicize her newfound identity as mother, actress, star.

Jessica, at this point, having been invited to parties of Misha's circle of superstar and émigré friends—the Czech director Milos Forman, the Soviet poet Joseph Brodsky—talked up her work in France with Decroux at the first possible chance. She was not a former model, she was a former mime. "It seemed to be the first thing out of her," remembered one acquaintance. "She was an extremely beautiful woman, but she had a look of ambition about her that was in contrast to her face." She seemed a "placid, quiet, and steely sort of girl," another recalled. Certainly, she had to hold her own against the claims of the possessive Russian community and the equally possessive dancing world. As the relationship strengthened, she pulled Misha away from the people he had turned to when he arrived in America, untutored in everything but ballet, just as, several years later, Sam Shepard would close out his old cronies under her influence.

In 1977 and 1978, however, into the vacuum of her love life fell Bob Fosse, another notorious ladies' man, which characteristic he was in the process of defining for *All That Jazz*. Though, as he put it in *American Film*, "with Jessica, I never knew where I stood. It was never spoken about, but I always knew I was waiting in line behind someone else she cared about, behind Mikhail or her husband. On my end, I never quite made her feel enough." It was, however, enough to end his six-year romance with dancer Ann Reinking. "Jessica's not an easy lady to know," Fosse said. He remembers the time he goaded her enough that she finally threw a drink in his face, and he thought: Good, I finally made her feel something.

But it was Fosse who finally got her back on celluloid. Lange had always hated auditions, and this part was written, literally, for her. Though the affair was over long before shooting began, Fosse's assessment of Lange's place is telling. She is conscience and chorus and untouchable beauty—she's the woman he's with when he dies and, one assumes, goes to heaven. She is perfectly still; her allure is deadly. "I saw this very attractive, sexual woman," Fosse said, "someone who was onto all my tricks and seemed to be very patient. So that was my idea of death—someone who was much smarter than me, who laughed at my little numbers."

The part for Jessica was a bit of a drag. Shooting at the end of the lengthy and overbudget film, Jessica sat swathed for hours in white gauze while designer Tony Walton and cameraman Guiseppe Rotunno created elaborate fantasy sequences. Lange, who had mastered a technique of deep relaxation which allowed her to stop and rest during the inevitable waits for actors, found herself stuck, upright and stiff, for hours. And she made no money from *All That Jazz*. But she learned. "Bob won't allow anything less than the truth," Lange said in a Fox press release. "One of the things that I learned through this experience—through Bob Fosse actually—was to get back to the subject. To explore what is really happening." She respected Fosse, she told reporters, and was glad she did it. It was also the most mimelike work she'd done yet.

The 20th Century–Fox publicity releases for *All That Jazz* bear the mark of Lange's frustrations with De Laurentiis's rewriting of her past. She is called "a former fashion model and a mime exponent," and her two years of study with Decroux are mentioned by name. "Ms. Lange is a firm believer in astrology and the paranormal," the reporter declaims, deeply serious. "After caresses from the 1,650-pound arms of her hairy lover threatened to crush life and limb," the release concludes somewhat dramatically, "her role in *All That Jazz* offers a pleasant diversion and restores her sense of cosmic balance."

No kidding. The role, unfortunately, did little for the balance of *All That Jazz*, which was a highly charged, entertaining, but overblown film in which Lange's part as an Angel of Death was one of the weakest. Ensconced in white gauze, bathed in blue light amid fantasy sets, Jessica smiles archly and speaks in dulcet tones of flirting reproval as the Fosse character spins on his way to a massive heart attack.

All That Jazz could perhaps summarize Lange's feelings about those years: doubt, uncertainty, depression about her work, her relationships, herself. Not, in fact, all that unusual for those in her generation who also had to adjust to the end of the sixties, to the end of an era and the loss of a certain kind of optimism. Waiting in the wings for her, not that she knew it, was a role that would establish her, in her thirties, as a premier actress of her generation, along with Meryl Streep, Jane Fonda, Sissy Spacek, Sally Field. And the title of her next film role would summarize the change quite adroitly: *The Postman Always Rings Twice*. She would have a second chance at fame.

13

RINGING TWICE

The cab ride from the airport took two hours and fifty dollars. It was dark in the North Carolina hills, and the cabbie got lost. His passenger, Bob Rafelson, had traveled to these Godforsaken parts to see an actress. A few months before, in Ohio, he had stomped off in a rage from the set of a big-budget motion picture named *Brubaker*, thereby freeing himself to do a longstanding project with his friend Jack Nicholson—the remake of *The Postman Always Rings Twice*. Rafelson, it was rumored, had chucked a folding chair at a studio executive sent out to urge him to move faster on *Brubaker*, which had fallen badly behind schedule.

Postman was a pet project, a dream project: Sven Nykvist would shoot; David Mamet, one of the most brilliant playwrights of his generation, was working on the screenplay; Jack, of course, *the* actor of his generation, would play the male half of the murderous couple who kill and then find themselves locked in revenge and hate. But Cora—Cora was the key. Cora was more than Cora, for this searing book by James M. Cain had a famous 1946 film version starring Lana Turner. Jack Nicholson would provide strong competition for John Garfield, but the right Cora would have to make audiences forget about Lana Turner—and that was no mean feat. Rafelson's

idea was to bring the sexuality inherent in the story out into the open, to make the film faithful to the lusty, vengeful spirit of the book.

While Rafelson wended his way in a cab through the hills, Jessica Lange was saying good-bye to her two co-stars from the play she somehow wound up doing in summer stock in Durham and Charlotte, North Carolina. It would be her first and last appearance on a stage. Lange had lived in utter solitude, except for her two dogs, all summer in a little town where she knew no one.

The play was an embarrassment; she had asked Rafelson, the director, not to see it. Every night it got harder to go on. "I took the part because I was broke," she explained to a reporter later. After three unproductive years, De Laurentiis had ended the exclusive seven-year contract with his former starlet from *King Kong*. "I made no money on *All That Jazz*. I hadn't worked in a long time. I just felt that I had to do something."

If Lange thought this would rid her of Fay Wraydom, she was wrong—the producers took it upon themselves to mention *King Kong* stardom in posters put up all over town. Jessica hated the play—*Angel on My Shoulder*, a daffy comedy by Stephen Levi about a mixed-up blonde. She was depressed. She sat in her hotel room and waited for Rafelson to show up.

Perhaps Rafelson, at about this point, thought back further —to a simpler day, when his unknown crew of hippies made movie history in low-budget, youth-oriented movies like *Easy Rider*, which he and his friend Bert Schneider produced, and *Five Easy Pieces*, which he directed and which made Jack a star. Or he might have thought back even to remember the Monkees, a prefabricated group in frank imitation of the Beatles, whom he had produced and directed. Their TV series made pop history, even a few hits, and led to his first film, *Head*, which Jack wrote. Nicholson and Rafelson—their lives were as intertwined as in-laws'.

Just before Jessica had departed for North Carolina and obscurity, Bob Rafelson had given her a call and asked if she'd ever read *The Postman Always Rings Twice*. She hadn't. Jessica ran out and bought a copy before she left.

James M. Cain had written the story at the height of the Depression, in 1934. Cora, his "hellcat," worked at her husband's diner. When a handsome young rake named Frank comes to visit, he spies Cora and stays. Eventually the two make brutal love ("Her lips stuck out in a way that made me want to mash them in for her," wrote Cain), then conspire, badly but ultimately successfully, to kill her husband. In the end, just as Cora reaches an inner peace with the knowledge of her pregnancy by Frank, Frank accidentally kills her in an automobile accident and is sent to the electric chair for the crime he didn't commit, rather than for the one he did.

Strange as it seemed, Bob liked auditioning people by talking to them, hanging out, seeing them in their native environs, even if that was North Carolina at midnight. He wouldn't have thought of Lange for the part if Nicholson hadn't pointed her out. Jack liked this actress. Jack had tested her in 1976 for one of his few directorial efforts, *Goin' South* (1977), in which he also starred. Her acting, actually, hadn't been that good in those screen tests with Jack—she was awkward, visibly nervous—but that was the strange thing: Jack was so much better with her in those tests than he'd been with anyone else. This jaded leading man, who out-acted, out-strutted, out-thought every actor and actress in Hollywood, seemed to click with the unformed, natural qualities of this beautiful woman just fresh from *King Kong*. Even Harold Schneider, *Goin' South*'s producer, had favored Lange for the part.

Jessica Lange, for her part, had liked Jack the moment she met him. At that first test together he had worked with her, patiently, gently, for four or five hours, despite an antsy crew and the obvious tension on the set. She'd never forgotten it. Mary Steenburgen got the part—on the strength of her Oscar for *Melvin and Howard*, undoubtedly. And the movie, it turned out, went nowhere. But Jack had sent her a dozen roses and a note: "I'm sure we will work together sometime soon. We will have lots of fun and make lots of money. Love, Jack." Well, roses are somewhat better than nothing, but not much, and Jessica Lange had chalked it up in the nice-try category.

Rafelson might have chuckled, on the two-hour drive, remembering the movies where Jack got his start. All those Roger Corman movies! *The Cry Baby Killer*, for Christ's sake. Everybody was a nobody once, as Fredric March put it in *A Star Is Born*. Sometimes these underrated actresses could do great stuff—just about the time this Lange girl was in *King Kong*, he'd put a television actress named Sally Field in a picture of his called *Stay Hungry*, written by his friend Charles Gaines. The picture hadn't done too well, but Sally Field had turned the critics around. Maybe he could do the same thing with this woman. She was clearly underutilized. She was thirty years old and hadn't made a decent picture yet.

When Rafelson finally arrived at her motel door, it was well after midnight, but Jessica wasn't the type to get upset. She smiled, they sat down to talk—and the phone rang. It was a private call, one that Jess had thought would arrive long after the director was gone. The director offered to move to the next room. No, don't bother, Lange said with a wave of her hand. He sat and watched.

"I watched her as she stayed on the phone a half-hour," Rafelson recalled in *New York*. It was as if, he felt, he had a long lens on her face. "There was something about the girl that was extremely poised. Her posture on the bed while she was talking made her seem like an incredible sensual lady."

It wasn't what she was saying, but how she said it that fascinated him. If he could somehow get this woman to be on screen the way she was there, that moment, on the motel bed, she would be "utterly, strikingly interesting," he thought. Her sexuality was inherent, her sensuality effortless.

Jessica hung up half an hour later, not knowing she had just passed her first test for the most coveted role of 1980. Or did she? Rafelson could detect no duplicity. "Or if there was," he said later, "it was so brilliant that I was unable to ascertain it. That's the hallmark of a great actress: If she can get it by me, she'll get it by the audience. But in fact, I thought there was none."

They talked long into the night. Then Rafelson returned to Hollywood. The task of interviewing potential Coras stretched before him. Some of Hollywood's hottest young actresses were crazy for the part: Cathy Moriarty, the throaty blonde of *Raging Bull*, Jill Clayburgh, and, in particular, Meryl Streep. None of them knew it, of course, but the standard they would be held to had been set in that little motel room with the two dogs.

To keep himself honest, Rafelson wrote Jessica's name as his first choice on a slip of paper with the date. His instinct was with her, though the casting process had only begun. Over the course of the summer, he had Lange take three separate screen tests. She looked better with each one.

For Jessica, these tests, like all auditions, were terrifying. She wished she weren't so obviously nervous, so blatantly timid. She thought carefully about every gesture, every motion. Rafelson noticed. "I saw little choices of behavior that were between her lines of dialogue and they gave me clues that she would inhabit Cora more elementally than any other actress." Also, interestingly, it was Jessica Lange's attitudes toward men that impressed Rafelson. She wasn't afraid of them. She didn't particularly need them; yet when they were around, she got them to do what she wanted. She had him lugging her baggage around the next morning, as she moved into another motel! Her Cora would be tough because Jessica was tough. But she would be sympathetic because she had an innate vulnerability that stemmed from the unself-consciousness of her allure. She was not afraid of sex, either, which was important for the film, which Nicholson and Rafelson planned to be as graphic as possible. "Jessica," Rafelson told the *Daily News* some years later, "is one of the few actresses I've ever met who is completely unself-conscious about her sexuality. That is not to say that she takes it for granted. But I observed, for instance, that when she sits down, both feet are planted on the ground; she doesn't cross her legs. There is almost a peasant quality about her that I found enormously attractive."

In the meantime, another movie, about as unlike *Postman* as could be imagined, materialized out of the blue when Lange's agent sent her a copy of *How to Beat the High Cost of Living*, a comedy that was to cast Lange with Susan Saint James and Jane Curtin. The plot concerned three frustrated middle-class housewives who, for various reasons, need money and decide to heist a shopping mall. The chief merit of the part, aside from being a very funny read, was that the producers already knew they wanted Lange to play it. "He [the agent] said we had a definite offer for this film," Lange recalled. "I didn't have to meet these people, I didn't have to read for them, nothing." The exact opposite, in other words, of this *Postman* ordeal. And she needed the money. And she could use the sheer experience of a more normal film shoot. This, after all, would only be her third.

Jessie laughed out loud when she read the script. She went on location in Oregon with Susan Saint James and Jane Curtin and they laughed some more, becoming great friends in the course of the shoot. Richard Benjamin played her obnoxious husband and they laughed. But the audiences didn't laugh. "*The High Cost* was a great deal of fun when we were on location in Oregon," Lange remembered. "But something was lost in all the different stages of finally putting a film together into final print." What was lost probably had something to do with a panicky sense of finishing the shooting in forty-five days. Robert Scheerer directed for American International-Filmways. The writer, Robert Kaufman, co-produced with Jerome Zeitman.

Ironically, for a film that opened and closed in a week the next summer to reviews that did nothing for Lange's or anyone else's reputation (Vincent Canby called it "a feeble housefly of a comedy"), *How to Beat the High Cost of Living* had some fairly impressive spinoffs. Curtin and Saint James later teamed up playing beleaguered divorced mothers again for the eighties CBS hit series "Kate & Allie." Also, a look back at this film gives a good idea of the endearing comedic style that won Lange an Academy Award in *Tootsie*. She has dignity, charm, and savvy; she has an impossible husband, just as in *Tootsie* she has an impossible boyfriend in Dabney Coleman; her nuances in the ensemble of women are impeccable; and, if nothing else, she is perhaps more cover-girl gorgeous than in any film before or since—perfect, classic looks.

As for *Postman*, Jessica waited on tenterhooks for five months. She read for Rafelson. She did video tests. Bob himself had taken her through a powerful love scene that takes place on Cora's kitchen table. Lange, of course, didn't know about any envelope from the summer before with her name on it. All she knew was that she didn't have the part yet, and "I didn't think there was anything more I could do to convince them I was Cora." Nicholson, for one, was already persuaded. Although Jack had begun, years before, with the idea of his then-lover, Michelle Phillips (of the Mamas and the Papas), for the part of Cora, by the time the film was actually a go project, Jessie was his favorite for the part. Long before the American public shared his opinion, Jack could see the potential stardom in Jessica Lange.

Bob Rafelson, by this point, had seen some 128 women. His eyes must have become bleary from looking at shapely blondes ready to throw themselves at his feet for the part; he could have counted them at night instead of sheep; but no one had taken his mind off Jessica Lange. There was just one more test before he could make up his mind: a screen test with Lange and Nicholson.

Jessica had not seen Nicholson since the tests for *Goin' South*. He had just finished *The Shining*. Jessica would be judged—not just for her acting ability, but this time for something indefinable but essential, the chemistry between two actors, actors who must play lovers and murderers, who must both attract and repel the audience and attract and repel each other. The sexual tension must be something very close to real, or the film would not work.

It worked. "Jack was great," Lange remembered. Though

he had dozens of ideas about what to do, "he didn't force them on me. His taste and intelligence were remarkable." The test, Lange knew, "was perfect." Bob fished out the envelope with her name in it and sent it by registered mail to her apartment in New York. She got the part. She was Cora.

14

POSTMAN

Fifteen minutes into *The Postman Always Rings Twice*, one of the most erotic love scenes on film takes place. It's on a kitchen table—a long, flour-covered table. Sunlight streams in. Jessica Lange, as Cora, knocks the bread knives, the fresh loaves, onto the floor. "Come on," she sneers at Jack Nicholson, impatient, fed up. "Come *on.*" He does.

If *The Postman Always Rings Twice* had managed to maintain the sputtering, fevered intensity of that moment, it would have made cinema history. As it is, the scene makes *The Postman Always Rings Twice* worth seeing at least once. The scene is explicit without being pornographic; Lange's cotton panties take on Nicholson's hands, then her own. She pounds and grunts, a woman seeking her own pleasure, and getting it.

Eroticism had always been the key to this remake, and *Postman* was awaited with great expectations, none greater than Jessica Lange's. A month after finishing *How to Beat the High Cost of Living*, she returned to the West Coast to start work on *Postman*. Her makeup woman was Dorothy Pearl. The hairdresser, Toni Walker, sheared her of her long blonde tresses, replacing them with a thirties perm with bangs that fell over her eyes like an ivory damask curtain. She put on some extra pounds, so she'd have "some weight on her," as Nicholson put it. She began walking, talking, thinking like this tough lady, this hungry, bored tigress locked up in a marriage with a man she'd never love. Authenticity was the key: Depression-era colors, a breathtaking Santa Barbara landscape, the deep blues of magic hour, and soft yellow lights of a simple home. Sven Nykvist, whose collaboration with Ingmar Bergman had made him one of the most respected cinematographers in the world, planned to capture the deep-focus feeling of the Depression-era black-and-white films with color film—taking advantage of the newest high-speed films, filters, and lenses which allowed for natural light and twilight shooting. Lana Turner's costumes had been in dazzling white. Jessica wore earth colors, cornflower-blue and brown. She was sexy in spite of the clothes, not because of them.

Jessica would look back on the experience of working with Bob Rafelson and Jack Nicholson—especially Jack—as one of the most rewarding periods of her professional life. She was the knowing innocent, they, the wizened guides. These two egos, whose battles on every collaboration made them swear never to work together again, sensed the fragile exterior of their new star, but saw through to the strength underneath. Had they been harsher with her, more demanding, at the outset, she would have fled. "I think if someone had said something negative to me at the start of the film, I would have closed up and shrunk away," Jessica said. But, sensing she could give more only because she gave more slowly, more subtly, than more professionally experienced actresses, they were gentle with her.

"It was such a positive experience with Jack and Bob just being given that opportunity," Jessica effused afterward to *New York* magazine's David Rosenthal. "Jack and Bob took my approach and my talents seriously and paid a great deal of attention to what I had to say about Cora. . . . Just as a woman, I understood her better—I shouldn't say better than they did, but differently. I felt they understood my ability and kept drawing things out." Amazingly, for once, Lange was not just following orders. Bob and Jack listened to her. "She was very helpful to me in terms of analyzing an overview of the whole picture," Nicholson said, "by bringing the attitudes of a very tough woman to her character."

While Sven and Bob shot the first scenes with Nicholson— the orange glow of his cigarette against a long blue stretch of twilight sky and highway—Jess stayed away from the set and filled in her portrait of Cora. She had never had such a multidimensional character to create before. Between Mamet's script and Cain's spare book, there was a lot of room for adding detail. From the beginning, Jessica told one interviewer, she had seen parallels between Cora's life and her own. Both were Midwesterners. Both had come to Hollywood in search of escape.

A passage in Cain's book—not in the script at all—between Cora and Frank gave Lange the skeleton for her character.

> Three years ago I won a beauty contest. [says Cora] I won a high school beauty contest, in Des Moines. That's where I lived. The prize was a trip to Hollywood. I got off the Chief with fifteen guys taking my picture, and two weeks later I was in the hash house."
> "Didn't you go back?"
> "I wouldn't give them the satisfaction."
> "And then?"
> "Then two years of guys pinching your leg and leaving nickel tips and asking how about a little party tonight. . . .

That was it, but it was enough. Jessica knew what that was like. "I saw how much she wanted a screen test," Jessica told one reporter shortly before *Postman* was released. "And what it would mean to her. Above all, she did not want to return to the Midwest as someone obscure." Ah, yes. A familiar feeling indeed, especially as Lange was returning to Paramount studios for the first time since her hurtful experience in *King Kong*. "Emotionally," Lange continued, "I could understand why. And I could understand why she had to get out of there, find a commitment." She visualized, painterlike, the moments in Cora's life. She surrounded her with a gallery from her own past: her own mother and father, her schools, her teachers, her adolescent anxieties and memories. She envisioned Cora's Christmases, the entries in her diary.

Jessica felt an "overwhelming sympathy with what she faced because I had been there too. There are certain traits that are in Cora that are in me. I worked as a waitress in Greenwich Village when I got back from Paris. Cora was a waitress in downtown Los Angeles when she got to California. I promised myself I would never lose control. I was logical, with a grasp of reality. I was not neurotic. Cora is the same."

Nicholson and Rafelson saw that no-nonsense quality in Lange. "She's like a cross between a delicate fawn and a Buick," quipped Nicholson. He called her Blinky, after her nearsightedness, a nickname she hated. Every day, the three of them would sit down and talk about the scenes ahead. Jess learned. She learned more from Nicholson than from any other actor she'd worked with. Jessica found herself part of an inner circle of driven, creative, meticulous filmmakers. It was an honor. Nicholson had just come from *The Shining*, with Stanley Kubrick, a film in which his character tries to murder his son with an axe. He was fascinated by sadomasochism, by what drives people to violence. Rafelson cared about these "unspeakably stupid, very very simple people" that were Cora and Frank.

Frank and Cora bungled their first murder attempt, tried it again, loved each other, hated each other, worked, loafed, had picnics, made love. As she had during the auditions, Jessica continued to put in her own little touches—staggering, slouching, purring, growling. During rushes, Bob would notice something she'd done that he'd missed on the set that day. Then he'd leap up out of his seat and shout: "Jess, you're brilliant." Even Fosse's attention hadn't been close to this kind of acclaim. Everyone told her how good she was. She felt like this was her true film debut, that the others had been false, groping, misbegotten starts.

Occasionally, Nicholson would snarl a nasty four-letter word or two to get her in the right mood (much as Dustin Hoffman's character met Teri Garr's in *Tootsie* before her audition to "enrage her"). Another scene, where she confesses her fear and guilt after the first murder attempt, required a long walk with Bob Rafelson before she could get it right. The walking would tire her out of being nervous, Rafelson figured.

The sex scenes were the heart of the film and took special consideration. A scene where the two lovers have just pushed the car over the edge and killed the husband required Jessie as Cora to be hit and her blouse torn by Jack (this was all in Cain's 1934 book). Jessica remembered it as the toughest one in the movie for her. The kitchen table scene, on the other hand, seemed "completely natural," she said. She, Bob, and Jack discussed the scene carefully before shooting. "When we were shooting them, it was always done in the best of taste. Everyone was very careful of everyone else's vulnerabilities and inhibitions." Bob's only specific direction was for them to use their hands to express the release of the pent-up desire between the two characters. He cleared the set of gaffers, makeup people, the continuity person, assistant directors, and the couple dozen or so other individuals who are the film actor's only real audience. Then he and Sven Nykvist took two 35-millimeter handheld cameras and began to shoot.

Did the kitchen scene bother Lange? "No, because it was an integral part of the story and I also knew going in that if you don't make it clear to the audience from the beginning that there's this overpowering bizarre chemistry between these two people, an obsession that changes the course of their lives—then the whole premise doesn't work."

The table scene, she knew, "is the key to the movie, and it had to contain the power and truth of what love does to these two people. . . . I can't tell if there is exaggeration because what I felt was the weird psychological twist, the moment when she stops fighting and beckons to him. I don't think Cora understood either. I didn't, but it happened. I believe that in a lifetime some incident, a word, a gesture, a look, can trigger that reaction, that can change everything."

"What happens in *Postman*," Rafelson said, "transcends the camera." The kitchen scene stopped being acting and became, rather, the filming of two people making love. Editing that scene, interestingly, was the same man, Graeme Clifford, who had edited another memorable and erotic love scene, between Julie Christie and Donald Sutherland in Nicholas Roeg's *Don't Look Now*.

Her dancer was far away, and Jessica was surrounded by the self-styled intelligentsia who filled Rafelson's social set. These people were Hollywood history of a certain kind—a group. While Lange had been studying mime, these folks had sat

around coffee houses and the beach at Venice, California, talking politics and movies in the same sentences, trying to create
a new cinema that reflected their generation. Perhaps they had
failed—they were now in their forties—but the prestige hung
about them like a faint lingering aroma. Besides Nicholson and
Bob and his wife, Toby Rafelson, the group included Laszlo
Kovacs and the two Schneider brothers, who, with Bob Rafelson, had formed BBS, the source of almost every important
"youth" movie in the late sixties and early seventies. As they'd
grown older, the group had grown to include serious writers
and artists, including the writer Jim Harrison, who became
one of Jessica's friends.

Jessica Lange has never said anything less than complimen-
tary about everyone and every scene in the film. Furthermore,
she steadfastly defended the film's love scenes in all her interviews—most of which she gave when she was nine months
pregnant: "I find nothing embarrassing in this film. The sexual
dynamism between the two is the most important thing in the
film. It is not gratuitous. It isn't something to be avoided. It's
there changing these two people before your eyes."

"The sensual and the erotic," Jessica said firmly, "is as basic
to life as it is to this film's story. I love this film and I enjoyed
acting in it. I have no dread, no sense of the negative. It was
a joyful process," she concluded—something she'd never said
about a film before. "And it has changed my whole feeling
about acting."

15

AND BABY MAKES TWO

By the time *Postman* opened, Jessica Lange had her first baby. Only two weeks before the March 20, 1981, debut, Jessie had walked the sixteen blocks to the Lenox Hill Hospital to have her baby naturally, her Lamaze instructor by her side, as Baryshnikov was dancing *Giselle* in Buffalo, New York. She walked because New York had been seized by a sudden snowstorm; even a woman in labor prefers walking to the perils of catching a cab in a snow-covered midtown Manhattan. The labor wasn't difficult for a first pregnancy. Misha jetted in the next day, a Friday, to see his healthy, eight-pound daughter. Buffalo audiences, deprived of their chance to see the superstar, were told that he had aggravated a knee injury (he had, in fact, been battling knee complications all that year). They named the girl Alexandra, after Misha's mother, a dressmaker who had abandoned Misha's family when he was thirteen. Shura would be the diminutive, even though Shura herself was not. She stayed in the hospital room right next to her mother, not in a nursery. "I want her right there with me," Lange explained.

Pregnancy and the birth of her child changed the world for Jessica Lange. Though she hadn't specifically planned on the baby, "emotionally," she said, "the timing was right." Of course, in terms of her long-delayed career, the timing appeared, at first, to be far from right. Long before a film is released, good word of mouth on a current or recent shoot can make a difference in the scripts that come in for future projects, and Jessica Lange was getting good word of mouth on *The Postman Always Rings Twice*. Reports of the steamy outtakes were making the rounds of Hollywood parties—but, more importantly, so was the news that the former Miss Kong (now the lover of the great Baryshnikov) was working with two of the most respected and innovative men in the business. Scripts arrived at her agent's daily. She was already in serious consideration for that most sought-after part, the title role in *Frances*.

At the end of the shoot, Rafelson praised Lange as "an enduring actress." "Nothing she does in the future will surprise me," he told one reporter. "After *Postman* she'll be able to act in anything. I believe she has more of an opportunity to become a star of more sensuality, intelligence, and overwhelming control than any other young actress around." Once again, Rafelson proved an apt judge of actors.

Returning from California that spring of 1980, Lange had stopped off in Minnesota to purchase 120 acres of birch and pine-forested land on which a two-story log cabin had already been built. The cabin was in Holyoke, Minnesota, near her parents and not far from Cloquet, where she'd graduated from high school. White birch and ash glistened in the sun; the lake had trout. In the summer, there would be blueberries. She traveled that summer with Baryshnikov, to Scandinavia, Paris, and, most importantly, to Cloquet. While George, her brother, and some of her male cousins took Misha on a tour of the local bars, her high-school girlfriends gave her a somewhat awkward baby shower. In Cloquet, they didn't quite know what to talk about at a shower for a mother-to-be who wasn't married. Not that anyone minded, really, but what do you talk about, then?

Everyone else had been married when they had babies. But then, Jess had always been a little different.

Though Jessica spoke often of how happy she was to be pregnant, the trappings of pregnancy annoyed her immeasurably. She refused to buy maternity clothes, conceding only for a pair of maternity pants, and received reporters for *Postman* publicity interviews in a magenta peasant blouse bursting at the belly. There were no pregnancy announcements until she obviously showed and the papers came out with the news, and there were no plans of marriage. In fact, she and Paco (remember Paco?) were in the middle of an ugly and painful divorce battle in the New York courts. Paco, now nearly blind and completely broke, was suing Lange for alimony. The papers got hold of the story and had a field day: STAR'S HUBBY BROKE & BLIND IN BOWERY FLOPHOUSE, wrote the *New York Post*. One of Paco's neighbors, an actress, made an irate phone call to the *Post*: "It's not a flophouse, it's a loft!" she yelled. "And he's not blind!" Lange's only public comment on the controversy was that she and Paco were on perfectly good terms. "He's as surprised by it as I am," she said.

The outcome of *Postman* came as a surprise as well. In a bevy of carefully written reviews, critics, who came to the film with all the high standards of James M. Cain, David Mamet, and Jack Nicholson in their minds, carefully compared their ideal of *The Postman Always Rings Twice* with what they saw —a pretentious, drawn-out, and surprisingly unfaithful rendition of the beloved book. Too bad for the film.

But not for Jessica. Jessica got on the map. If anyone was miscast, it was Nicholson, who, according to some critics, seemed, to them, too old and physically unappealing to have attracted the lusty Cora—a criticism that infuriated Lange. For many critics, Jessica Lange's performance, not Nicholson's was "the best reason for seeing this *Postman*," as Pauline Kael wrote. "She stands and walks with her rump out proudly. It dominates the movie. You have no trouble believing that Frank has to grab her . . . she's both seraphic and steamy."

"It's from Jessica Lange's Cora that [the film] gets its life. . . . Lange makes her an understandable victim," wrote the *Los Angeles Times*. "There's something still girlish about Lange's Cora, whose sensuality registers with men before other women even notice it." "Jessica Lange deserves to be remembered as Cora," wrote Richard Corliss in *Time*. "Her fierce commitment makes this *Postman* something more than the sum of its private parts."

Taken now, with an eye to watching two remarkable performances and an attitude about an American classic, this film has much to offer. It is, truly, beautiful. And it did make money, in the end, in worldwide distribution. Jack Nicholson told a *Film Comment* reviewer in 1985: "If you ran a question through this industry about *The Postman Always Rings Twice*, most people would surmise that it wasn't successful. That is not true. I know it made money because I received overages, so it must have grossed about as much as *Chinatown* and much more than *Carnal Knowledge*. But people are anxious to disqualify it."

And so, on to *Frances*.

It was ironic that just as Jessica Lange was about to dive into the maelstrom of Frances Farmer's psyche, that dark, embittered, caldron of outrage, she was, herself, more at peace than she had ever been. She had given birth. Her on-again, off-again relationship with Baryshnikov, the subject of so much gossip and speculation in the past six years, had settled into, if not wedded bliss, at least the status of a recognized couple. Misha continued to receive the requisite plaudits in his new and very demanding job as director of the American Ballet Theater, but his career no longer overwhelmed hers. And her child fulfilled her in unexpected ways. "I never knew being a mother would make me so happy," she said, glowing. At the age of thirty-one, she found herself thrust into the role of quintessential and thoroughly satisfied working mom, talking nannies and acting in the same breath.

With her work life and home life so full, Lange seldom went out, abandoning the practices of her earlier starlet days, when she'd been photographed dancing at Studio 54 with Bob Fosse. She waited, instead, with Shura at Misha's penthouse apartment where the two had finally consolidated households. Before *Frances* and *Tootsie*, Lange could still wheel Shura through Central Park unnoticed. Without makeup, a pair of oversized tinted glasses slipping down on her nose, wearing khakis, a man-sized shirt, and Minnetonka moccasins, she looked like an atypically unpretentious new mother in one of the world's most expensive neighborhoods.

On weekends, Misha, the baby, and Lange retreated to Misha's large stone house in Sherman, Connecticut, where the ninety acres of woods reminded the expatriate dancer of the woods outside Moscow, and where his best friend Milos Forman was only a half hour's drive away. The stone house, built in a Tudor style of the 1920s, had walls twelve inches thick, four working fireplaces, four bedrooms, and two baths. A caretaker, his wife, and two children lived in a cottage nearby. Jessica had planted hundreds of tulip bulbs the previous spring, and they bloomed for the first time in the spring of 1981 as she awaited the start of *Frances* rehearsals. She and Misha shopped for English and French country peasant antiques in western Connecticut. They rode horses, fished for trout, and went skeetshooting—very much like a pair of landed gentry, albeit for only brief weekends at a time. In less busy days, Lange had refinished the kitchen cabinets to their original wood by hand.

Her refinishing days were behind her now. In May, Jessica's oldest sister Ann took some vacation time from her job as an art director in Minneapolis and she and Jessica took Shura to the Cannes Film Festival, where Rafelson had persuaded Lange that an appearance would help to promote *Postman*, even though the film was not in competition. Sure enough, the film, a failure financially in the United States, was successfully plugged as an art film and did well in Europe. On the arms of Nicholson and Rafelson, resplendent in white, Lange played the movie star by night while Ann, an experienced mother of four (including daughter Jessica), baby-sat. During the sun-washed days, Jessica steered her celebrity offspring in her carriage past hordes of paparazzi. Baby Shura made her newsprint debut at Cannes, aged three months.

Lange, in fact, was Frances Farmer's opposite. Not merely in the sense that, emotionally, she had found fulfillment through the love of a child and a man, but professionally as well. Frances Farmer battled poorly, stumbled, lost her way in the city of dreams. Not Jessica. She had taught herself. She understood the entertainment press, now. She gave the right kind of interviews. Far from being a victim of Hollywood, she played the Hollywood game with skill. "She got the roles when she was a nobody that everybody who was a somebody wanted," one observer noted. In two short years, she would become the first woman actress in four decades to be nominated for both Best Supporting Actress and Best Actress. She was nobody's victim.

No, she was really, of all her characters, the most like Cora. Cora with the iron will, made powerful by sex, who wouldn't go back, who wouldn't give her small town the satisfaction of knowing she had failed. "Above all," Jessica had said, "Cora did not want to return to the Midwest as someone obscure." Well, who would? In the Midwest, there are no battles worth winning, something the Coras and Jessicas of the world have always known.

16

HOME

C loquet is a town with a subtext: wood. Lumber defines the economy, sparing Cloquet from some of the ravages of the Iron Range depression in shipping and mining. The Diamond Matches factory and a substantial sawmill greet the visitor coming in from Interstate 35, just a few miles south of Duluth. The local weekly paper is the *Pine Knot,* the high-school yearbook the *White Pine.*

Before Jessica Lange put Cloquet on the map, the town's most famous exports were professional hockey goalies. One Barbara Payton, born in 1937, was Cloquet's only previously known contribution to Hollywood. In the little community, Lange's maternal grandfather, George Sahlman, was an important local citizen. He had served a term in the state legislature, owned a clothing store and a local tavern, headed a nearby oil company, and held the known record for winter golfing at the local country club, having played eighteen rounds one frigid day on December 17, 1957. When Dorothy and Al Lange brought their family back to Cloquet in 1966, Jessie was a little less of a new kid than in the many other towns they'd lived in. In Cloquet, she had a clearly defined niche as one of George Sahlman's granddaughters, and her cousins, the Pelskins, were well known in the town as well.

Jessica Phyllis Lange was born in Cloquet on April 20, 1949, in the same town where her maternal grandparents had met years before at a dance in the pavilion. Both grandparents had been born, coincidentally, in the same town in Finland. Her paternal grandfather, an orphan, had migrated to St. Paul from Poland. "He made a little money and he bought a map of the states, and every place that had a star on the map, he followed," Lange said in *Vanity Fair*. There he met Lange's maternal grandmother, whose father owned the sandstone quarry where he was working. Her paternal grandmother came from Friesland, a proud, sea-faring province in the northern Netherlands.

Her Finnish grandparents, the Sahlmans, were an important fixture in Dorothy and Albert Lange's family. Both had, at one time, been active in labor theater during the Depression in northern Minnesota.

Nonetheless, Jessica's first memory is of the Gulf of Mexico, drifting from shore, way over her head in an inner tube. Jessie was then two years old and already getting as far away from terra cognita as she could. On shore was her father, working in the South during the Korean War, in one of the eighteen towns he would move his family to before Jessica, his third daughter, was in high school. On shore were two big sisters, Ann and Jane, and a newborn baby brother, George, her comrades in these endless moves, and, watching over them, her mother, Dorothy. Her father worked in various jobs—as a school gym teacher, gas station operator, Ford dealer, regional salesman for Conoco—finally working part-time for Burlington Northern Railroad. "We lived pretty much like gypsies," Jessica said.

Lange's family is a subgroup of the Midwest, a fascinating genre usually overlooked in the more familiar stereotypes of the Midwest as a land of wholesome, earnest, settled farmers and corner drugstore owners. There have always been, in the Middle West, men tossed about by uncertain ambitions, men who tussle bitterly with fate, men who repeat the same mistakes in ten different small towns, dragging behind them the hapless innocents who appear on this dreamscape almost as an afterthought. What they want is always in the future—each town, each profession turns out to be wrong.

Throughout the Midwest, too, are patient, weary mothers who long for roots for themselves and their babies; but who, instead, during the same years that they married the soldiers and began repopulating the planet, picked up, packed, and lugged their way behind their husband's dreams from one small town to the next.

The psychiatrists call it a fear of success; the folk tales name him a dreamer. To little Jessie, it was just her father, the father you don't think to question, the father whose powerful dreams ricocheted the family across the South and Midwest. Her father, she told a *Washington Post* reporter in 1977, "just liked to move around a lot. I don't know why. . . . " The only center of gravity was her own imagination.

"When you have a powerful, charismatic person in your life, you are drawn to this person," Lange said in discussing the relationship between Frances Farmer and her powerful mother. "My own father was like that. Acceptance or rejection depends on that parent." On the other hand, her mother was "incredible, just an incredible mother." "I don't know how Mother would just pack the four of us and follow him," Jessica said. "Because every two years he was changing jobs."

All these moves meant that Lange was eternally the new kid in school. A shy girl, walking into a new classroom was always terrifying for her. "I wasn't good at making friends," Lange recalls, "and when after a year or so, I made a few friends, I knew we'd be leaving. Of course we did, so the process continued. I rationalize it to myself these days by saying, it conditioned me for my later life, conditioned me not to make permanent connections, at least, not too quickly or too often."

Some legacy. Having to rely only on yourself and your brother and sisters for support tends to create a kind of double negative in relationships. On the one hand, you learn to be the new kid—to say hi to everybody, to stay out of trouble, to figure out what the rules are at this new school, and learn to play by them. The new kid is always, inherently, an actor—a mimic, a mime. But the circle of people you really trust remains very, very small. You don't trust your own ability to get the attention of strangers—and yet you come to expect that attention as a sign of how well you're doing. But you rely, inside, on the certain knowledge of that little clump of people who will never leave you—your mom, your dad, your sisters, your brother. Who is family? Those people who loved you before you did anything worth loving, who love you just the same when the rest of the world decides you did.

To find the roots you have to go back another generation—not to these wandering sons, who never find a way to replace home, but to home itself—to the grandparents and brothers and sisters and their children; the people who never move more than thirty miles from their birthplaces in counties where everyone with the same last name is related. The foundation for Jessica was in her beloved maternal grandparents, the Sahlmans, whose seventy-year marriage ended only with Grandpa Sahlman's death at ninety-four in June of 1985. Her grandparents remained, until George Sahlman's death, "the hub of the

family," Lange would say in publicizing *Country*. "Clan" became an oft-repeated word in those later interviews with
Lange, the importance of clan.

Jessica, said her father, "is very determined. She was like that
from the day she was born. She made up her mind to make a
success of it and she did." At age seven she bashed into a
parking meter, from whence she got her little "boxer's nose"
—one that De Laurentiis would want changed. A big kid,
painfully shy, with uninteresting dark brown hair and heavy
eyebrows, she was the ugly duckling—the lost kid in a family
of four. Her oldest sister Ann, five years older than Jessica, is
a painter, and became an art director in Minneapolis (locals
insist that she's the real beauty of the family); Jane, two years
Jessica's senior, also a dreamer and traveler, lived for the last
twelve years on a Newfoundland schooner with her daughter.
Baby George, three years younger than Jessica—and reportedly quite a cutie himself—is still single and a commercial pilot.

Though shy, Jessie could be heartlessly cruel when crossed
by a sister or cousin, according to David Rosenthal's profile in
Rolling Stone. "My fear of unpleasant things when I was a
child, avoidance at all costs, was so great," Lange recalled in
The New York Times, that "if I anticipated an embarrassing
moment coming up for a character on a television show, I had
to leave the room. That kind of 'I won't say anything' settles
in your heart and fills the well of rage. I don't let it happen
anymore."

She escaped into fantasy lands of her own creation. "I lived
pretty much in a fantasy world growing up," she recalled.
Gone With the Wind and *Wuthering Heights*—the books and the
movies—provided her with role models of escape. "I saw *Gone
With the Wind* at least fourteen times," Lange recalled. She

memorized the dialogue between Scarlett and Melanie and played both their parts. She received letters from Rhett, written by herself. Heathcliff became her model of an ideal love—not such a great role model there, and one it would take her some years to shed. "For me, movies had been a great escape. They were part of a romantic vision of life," she said. She played by herself for hours, hearing the sound of the loons from a nearby lake. Occasionally, to her mortal embarrassment, she would be caught in one of her four- or five-way conversations with these movie characters.

She felt "trapped, almost suffocated," by Minnesota. "When I was younger, I used the country as an escape," she said. "I was terribly shy and that made me avoid people." Nor was hers the most idyllic of families. Lange coveted the possessions of friends who had more money. Her parents quarreled. Her mother and aunt "let things slide by," and Jessie learned from their example. Her retreat was her imagination; her belief that her life would change sustained her.

"I knew," Lange explained, "that somewhere along the line my life was bound to take a drastic change. I knew there was definitely something in store for me. I had that feeling from the time I was very young. I always felt a certain amount of restlessness there, a yearning."

By the time Lange had graduated from high school, "it was really percolating. My school spirit left a great deal to be desired. I definitely wasn't the popular girl, homecoming queen or cheerleader or anything like that. A lot of people didn't like me or my attitude. I just wanted to get out of there and I think they sensed that. I thought their life of small-town politics sucked, basically, and I didn't like their cheerleaders or their social setup."

The Jessie Lange that her high-school pals remember, how-

ever, was not a rebel, but a part of a large, closely knit crowd
that still identifies themselves as the Class of '67. "We were
about sixty or seventy people," remembers one friend, "and we
all considered ourselves something of a rebel—it was that generation." Jessie was cast as the female lead in the senior class
play, *Rebel Without a Cause*. It was her first exposure to acting,
and she was eagerly involved. But the play never made it to
opening night, cut short by a bizarre incident. A girl was found
knifed to death in the high-school band room a few days before
the play was due to open. The murder turned out to have been
a lover's quarrel that involved two brothers, and the shock was
enough to make the school authorities close the play, ostensibly
because it, too, contained a knife scene. Bitterly disappointed,
Jessie gave up on acting until her mid-twenties.

Jessie painted, decorating the 1967 high-school prom with
psychedelic swirls of color. She was also a reporter for the
school paper and an honor student. Jessie Lange was remembered as something of a maverick, the one who first experi-
mented with the ideas and fashions just then seeping into the
Iron Range from San Francisco and Greenwich Village. A
long autobiography written for a high-school teacher was such
a scathing indictment of everything she'd grown up with that
the teacher admonished her not to give up on all traditional
values.

In all of her interviews—through *King Kong, Frances, Country*—Lange mentions an irreducible sense of loneliness—a
sense that there was something more out there, waiting for her,
something she couldn't get in Cloquet or any one of the eighteen other towns the family lived in. It was there in her favorite
stories, the elemental conflict of the girl whose dreams com-
pelled her to leave what she loved. In *Wuthering Heights'*

Kathy, in *Gone With the Wind*'s Scarlett O'Hara, the girl leaves home behind to create a new world for herself, but is nonetheless always in conflict with her home, to which she invariably returns—at a cost. "Even during periods when I was really happy," Lange remembered, "I felt cut off somehow, that I wasn't quite inside things. It was real hard."

"My most powerful connection is to Minnesota," Lange intoned recently, "to that part of the land. I have a certain love for it I have for nothing else. I feel better there than anywhere else in the world." But that was not the Jessie Lange who sat on the front porch on summer evenings as a teenager. Then, the crickets hummed, the dogs barked, and Jessie would sit there "filled with such yearnings I thought I would explode." If she stayed there one more day, it would kill her, she thought. "I couldn't wait to get out," she said.

She got out.

FILMOGRAPHY

KING KONG (1976)
Paramount Pictures
Producer: Dino De
   Laurentiis
Dierctor: John Guillermin
Screenplay: Lorenzo Semple
Starring: Jeff Bridges,
   Charles Grodin, and
   introducing Jessica Lange

ALL THAT JAZZ (1979)
20th-Century–Fox
Producer: Robert Alan
   Aurthur
Director: Bob Fosse
Screenplay: Robert Alan
   Aurthur and Bob Fosse
Starring: Roy Scheider,
   Jessica Lange, Ann
   Reinking, and Leland
   Palmer

*HOW TO BEAT THE
HIGH COST OF LIVING*
   (1980)
American
   International-Filmways
Producer: Jerome Zeitman
   and Robert Kaufman
Director: Robert Scheerer
Screenplay: Robert Kaufman
Starring: Jane Curtin, Susan
   St. James, Jessica Lange,
   and Richard Benjamin

*THE POSTMAN ALWAYS
RINGS TWICE* (1981)
Paramount Pictures
Producer: Andrew
   Braunsberg
Director: Bob Rafelson
Screenplay: David Mamet.
   Based on the novel by
   James M. Cain.
Starring: Jack Nicholson
   and Jessica Lange

FRANCES (1982)
Universal Pictures
Producer: Jonathan Sanger
Director: Graeme Clifford
Screenplay: Eric Bergren,
Christopher De Vore and
Nicholas Kazan
Starring: Jessica Lange, Sam
Shepard, and Kim Stanley

TOOTSIE (1982)
Columbia Pictures
Producer: Sydney Pollack
and Dick Richards
Director: Sydney Pollack
Screenplay: Larry Gelbart
and Murray Schisgal.
Based on a story by Don
McGuire and Larry
Gelbart.
Starring: Dustin Hoffman
and Jessica Lange

COUNTRY (1984)
Touchstone Films
Producer: Jessica Lange and
William Wittliff
Director: Richard Pearce
Screenplay: William Wittliff
Starring: Jessica Lange and
Sam Shepard

CAT ON A HOT TIN
ROOF (1984)
Showtime/American
Playhouse
Director: Jack Hofsiss
Written by Tennessee
Williams
Starring: Jessica Lange,
Tommy Lee Jones, Rip
Torn, and Kim Stanley

SWEET DREAMS(1985)
Tristar
Producer: Bernard Schwartz
Director: Karel Reisz
Screenplay: Robert
Gretchell
Starring: Jessica Lange, Ed
Harris, and Ann
Wedgeworth